MW00582217

SOUND GENERATION

The Resonant Voices of Teen Girls

www.writegirl.org

A WriteGirl Publication

ALSO FROM WRITEGIRL PUBLICATIONS

Emotional Map of Los Angeles: Creative Voices from WriteGirl
You Are Here: The WriteGirl Journey
No Character Limit: Truth & Fiction from WriteGirl
Intensity: The 10th Anniversary Anthology from WriteGirl
Beyond Words: The Creative Voices of WriteGirl
Silhouette: Bold Lines & Voices from WriteGirl
Lines of Velocity: Words that Move from WriteGirl
Untangled: Stories & Poetry from the Women and Girls of WriteGirl
Nothing Held Back: Truth & Fiction from WriteGirl
Pieces of Me: The Voices of WriteGirl
Bold Ink: Collected Voices of Women and Girls
Threads
Pens on Fire: Creative Writing Experiments for Teens from WriteGirl (Curriculum Guide)

IN-SCHOOLS PROGRAM ANTHOLOGIES

Unstoppable: Creative Voices of the WriteGirl & Bold Ink Writers In-Schools Programs
These Moments: The Creative Voices of the WriteGirl In-Schools Program
Ocean of Words: Bold Voices from the WriteGirl In-Schools Program
Words & Curiosity: Creative Voices of the WriteGirl In-Schools Program
This Is My World: Creative Voices of the WriteGirl In-Schools Program
Ready for the Next Chapter: Creative Voices of the WriteGirl In-Schools Program
No Matter What: Creative Voices from the WriteGirl In-Schools Program
So Much to Say: The Creative Voices of the WriteGirl In-Schools Program
Sound of My Voice: Bold Words from the WriteGirl In-Schools Program
This Is Our Space: Bold Words from the WriteGirl In-Schools Program
Ocean of Words: Bold Voices from the WriteGirl In-Schools Program
Reflections: Creative Writing from Destiny Girls Academy
Afternoon Shine: Creative Writing from the Bold Ink Writers Program
    at the Marc & Eva Stern Math and Science School
Words That Echo: Creative Writing from Downey, Lawndale and Lynwood
    Cal-SAFE Schools
The Landscape Ahead: Creative Writing from New Village Charter High Schools
Sometimes, Just Sometimes: Creative Writing from La Vida West and
    Lynwood Cal-SAFE Programs
Everything About Her: Creative Writing from New Village High School
Visible Voices: Creative Writing from Destiny Girls Academy
Now That I Think About It: Creative Writing from Destiny Girls Academy
Look at Me Long Enough: Creative Writing from Destiny Girls Academy

ACCLAIM FOR WRITEGIRL PUBLICATIONS

Praise for *Sound Generation: The Resonant Voices of Teen Girls*

"Words alone are mostly meaningless. Words strung together can have rhythm and power and saliency. The symphony of the teenaged experience is precisely why WriteGirl exists — to capture the sloppiness and the art of being alive."

> – Heather Hach Hearne, screenwriter of *Freaky Friday* and
> *What to Expect When You're Expecting* and librettist for
> *Legally Blonde: The Musical*

"Fearless, raw and melodic — these poems and stories stand up and belt out: 'I am here.' The writing on these pages is not remarkable 'for a teen.' It's remarkable — full stop. Each voice in *Sound Generation* hums with verve and veracity."

> – Rachel Caris Love, screenwriter of *Blindspot*

"WriteGirl is an incredible organization. I have been amazed at the quality of the work these girls produce. I congratulate the staff on working so hard to provide these young ladies with a safe space and the tools that they need to succeed."

> – Keiko Agena, actress, *Gilmore Girls* and *13 Reasons Why*,
> and author of the forthcoming "artist workbook"
> *No Mistakes* (Tarcher/Perigree, summer 2018)

Praise for *Emotional Map of Los Angeles: Creative Voices from WriteGirl*

"It is a gift to explore Los Angeles through the eyes of these brave and talented young women. I'm awed and inspired by the way this collection captures the heart, nerves and soul of our city. We have so much to look forward to from the next generation of L.A. writers. This book is a remarkable and unforgettable trip. Prepare to be stirred."

> – Kami Garcia, #1 *New York Times* bestselling coauthor
> of *Beautiful Creatures* and author of *Unbreakable*

"The only thing more inspiring than WriteGirl, the organization, is the girls themselves. Their process is a combination of work and play, craft and self-exploration. The results are kind of mind-boggling!"

> – Josann McGibbon, screenwriter of *Descendants*, *Runaway Bride*,
> *The Starter Wife*

"I was reintroduced to the city where I was born and raised courtesy of these talented girls and their unique stories, perspectives and insights. Their talent will inspire the reader and leave no doubt as to what a WriteGirl is capable of, as long as she has a pen and some paper."

    – Kelley Turk, television writer

"When I read these poems, I am impressed by the strong sense of place, and how WriteGirl mentors have helped these young writers discover their city and their homes because deep roots foster tall dreams."

    – Xochitl-Julisa Bermejo, poet and co-founder of Women Who Submit

"Getting to see Los Angeles through the eyes of these young girls reminded me how big the small things that make up our lives really are. These WriteGirl authors plucked them out and treated them as beautiful bookmarks inside their own story. I was more than happy to disappear into these private moments and share in their experiences as if they were my own…if only for a page of two."

    – Courtney Turk, television writer

"There's nothing like a jolt of beautiful, authentic voices to inspire and delight… WriteGirl gets down life. We get to share in that raw power."

    – Rita Hsiao, co-writer, *Mulan, Toy Story 2*

"The remarkably assured and soul-stirring pieces in this anthology are filled with tender introspection, fierce engagement with the world, and precise and intimate knowing. All testify to the fact that WriteGirl is succeeding in its mission to empower girls through writing. These girls have voices, and they know how to use them. Readers, prepare to be enthralled."

    – Marisa Silver, novelist and short story writer, *Mary Coin* and
      The God of War

Praise for *You Are Here: The WriteGirl Journey*

"The name could just as easily be "Write, Girl!" — an exhortation for a young woman to take her life, her future, her sense of self into her own hands by putting a pen there. Nothing has the sheer human power to change minds and hearts that a simply and beautifully wrought sentence has. Write, girls!"

    – Patt Morrison, *Los Angeles Times* columnist, radio host for
      KPCC, best-selling author

Praise for *No Character Limit: Truth & Fiction from WriteGirl*

"Adolescents reading this anthology will recognize themselves in the words. Aspiring wordsmiths can use the works as models for their own writing or try their turn at the various exercises in the book."

— *School Library Journal*

"Showcases work by the girls and their mentors that explore universal feelings about friendship, family and adolescence."

— *Ms. Magazine* (Great Reads for Winter 2013)

"In this book, what these girls have to say makes us laugh at times, and other times makes us want to cry. But their words always make us believe. These girls understand the power of words."

— Meg Cabot, author, *The Princess Diaries, Allie Finkle's Rules for Girls, Size 12 and Ready to Rock*

"The writings in *No Character Limit* are bold and passionate. The words grab you, shake you and invade your brain, but most of all they make you grateful — grateful that these girls are writing, sharing with us their unique perspectives on the human condition."

— Jennifer Crittenden, writer/producer, *The New Adventures of Old Christine, Arrested Development, Everybody Loves Raymond*

Praise for *Intensity: The 10th Anniversary Anthology from WriteGirl*

"I have never owned a WriteGirl anthology that didn't eventually make the rounds of my friends. The writing is fine writing, and that the authors are young writers makes no difference. Art is art. Good writing is good writing. And every emotion finds genuine expression."

— Eloise Klein Healy, Poet Laureate of Los Angeles

"Many writers think, 'I can't,' or 'I'm not good at this,' or 'I don't know how to spell the words.' But the best way a writer can overcome self-doubt is to keep writing. These girls started with a few words and the seed of an idea. With WriteGirl's encouragement, each girl allowed the words to keep coming until her idea grew into an essay, a story or a poem. What do writers do? They write. And how lucky we are to have these writers' words and ideas to inspire us!"

— Carole King, GRAMMY® Award-winning singer and songwriter

Praise for *Beyond Words: The Creative Voices of WriteGirl*

"Powerful and strong, raw and vulnerable — these are the voices of girls who demand to be heard. Girls who know their words have real meaning, in a world that can often feel anything but real. WriteGirl's latest anthology, *Beyond Words*, is proof of their conviction. You will not only hear them, but you'll never forget them."

— Kami Garcia, *New York Times* bestselling author of *Beautiful Creatures*

"Writing has been my life, and I work very hard at it. Having a group like WriteGirl is an amazing help to those who love the craft. The mentoring of the young girls is a wonderful way to pair the professional with the new writers to show them how to hone their skills and have a successful career doing so. The excerpts written by these girls are inspiring and show genuine talent. I give a big thumbs-up to WriteGirl and to those who are working hard to do what they love so much."

— Diane Warren, GRAMMY® Award-winning songwriter,
"Because You Loved Me"

"WriteGirl is a life-changing program that reaches out and supports young women to express themselves through writing. The dedicated mentors who do the hard work with them are guardian angels. And I suspect it is as life-changing for them as it is for the young authors."

— Naomi Foner, screenwriter, *Bee Season, Losing Isaiah, Running on Empty*

"Cheers to Keren Taylor for coming up with the dream of giving teenage girls a voice, and then creating an organization that made her dream a reality. Cheers also for her hardworking staff, and the dedicated volunteers and mentors of WriteGirl for enabling teenage girls to wrestle the truth of their lives, their hearts and souls, into literary form on the page. And another round of cheers for *Beyond Words*, the latest addition to WriteGirl's growing library of award-winning anthologies."

— Barbara Abercrombie, UCLA Extension creative writing instructor, author,
*Kicking in the Wall: A Year of Writing Exercises, Prompts, and Quotes to
Help You Break Through Your Blocks and Reach Your Writing Goals*

"The WriteGirls are woman warriors of the pen. To read their poems and stories is to be heartened by their wonderful, inspiring, regenerating powers."

— Maxine Hong Kingston, author, *The Woman Warrior,
The Fifth Book of Peace, I Love a Broad Margin to My Life*

Praise for *Silhouette: Bold Lines & Voices from WriteGirl*

"WriteGirl is essential to helping our young women know how important their thoughts and feelings, not just their looks and bodies, are. Right on, girls — WriteGirl!"

> — Nikki Giovanni, poet, *Bicycles: Love Poems, Blues: For All the Changes, Quilting the Black-Eyed Pea*

Praise for *Listen to Me: Shared Secrets from WriteGirl*

"The wit and wisdom found inside *Listen to Me* comes in whispers, shouts, giggles, cries, chortles, inner ahas and other creative noises — proving once again that the voices of women and girls are as rich and varied as a great symphony. WriteGirl's newest anthology hits your funny bone in new places, strums your heart strings and strikes just the right chords to make your imagination sing. Listen to me, do yourself a favor and pay attention to what's being said in *Listen to Me*."

> — Jane Wagner, writer/producer/director, *The Incredible Shrinking Woman, The Search for Signs of Intelligent Life in the Universe*

"I love hearing the new voices in these pages. I've had the pleasure of being part of one of WriteGirl's workshops. Now when I meet a young woman in her teens who asks for advice on becoming a writer, I instantly say, 'Have you heard of WriteGirl? Get involved with them immediately!'"

> — Robin Swicord, screenwriter, *The Curious Case of Benjamin Button, Memoirs of a Geisha;* screenwriter/director, *The Jane Austen Book Club*

Praise for *Lines of Velocity: Words that Move from WriteGirl*

"Unlike many such anthologies, this collection includes the work of experienced mentors…as well as the teen participants. The result is a dynamic exchange of shared prompts, ideas and projects. The writing is at times hilarious. At other times, it is heartbreaking. This anthology is sure to be picked up by aspiring young writers as well as educators looking for inspired samples and interactive exercises."

> — *School Library Journal*

"*Lines of Velocity* sparks with the lively intelligence of gifted young writers well on their way to discovering the power of language. If I'd had the WriteGirl experience at the onset of my formative years, who knows? I might be a Pulitzer Prize winner by now."

> — Suzanne Lummis, poet and teacher, *In Danger (The California Poetry Series)*

Praise for *Untangled*: *Stories & Poetry from the Women and Girls of WriteGirl*

"This fifth anthology is a worthwhile and highly motivational compendium of poetry, short stories, nonfiction and dramatic excerpts from both students and teachers. Including great topic suggestions, writing experiments and insight into the creative process, this volume is a perfect fit for the high school classroom. Sharp observations abound…unconventional writing exercises…motivational quotes…nonstop inspiration."

    – *Publishers Weekly*

"*Untangled* gives me hope, riles me up, revs me up, makes me sad, makes me happy, makes me want to write, and makes me want to read. All I ever think about is how to make more young women want to share their voices with the world — and WriteGirl, plus this anthology — are actually doing it. There's nothing cooler than jumping into the worlds of these young women as well as the minds of the brilliant women who mentor them. Untangled rocks!"

    – Jill Soloway, writer/producer, *United States of Tara;* author,
      Tiny Ladies in Shiny Pants

"The writing here, always moving and sometimes painful, displays freshness, an exuberant inventiveness, and — surprisingly — a hard-won wisdom. Some of these young women will undoubtedly grow up to be poets, journalists and novelists. All of them have already learned to write honestly and with conviction."

    – Benjamin Schwarz, literary and national editor, *The Atlantic*

Praise for *Nothing Held Back*: *Truth & Fiction from WriteGirl*

"For these girls (and their mentors) writing is a lens, a filter, a way to cut through the nonsense and see the possibilities. …[*Nothing Held Back*] suggests that reports of literacy's death have been greatly exaggerated, that language remains a transformative force."

    – David Ulin, editor, *Los Angeles Times Book Review*

Praise for *Pieces of Me*: *The Voices of WriteGirl*

"Wow! I couldn't stop reading this. Talk about goosebumps! This book will shock you — and make you think — and make you FEEL — all at the same time!"

    – R.L. Stine, author, *Goosebumps* and *Fear Street* series

"All the boldness, unselfconsciousness, lack of vanity and beautiful raw talent that is usually tamped down by adulthood bursts from these pages and announces a formidable new crop of young writers."

> — Meghan Daum, author, *Life Would Be Beautiful If I Lived in That House* and *My Misspent Youth*

"*Pieces of Me* is a riveting collection of creative writing produced by girls and women with enormous talent. On every page you'll encounter fresh voices and vibrant poems and stories that pull you into these writers' worlds, into the energy of their lives."

> — Vendela Vida, author, *Away We Go, Let the Northern Lights Erase Your Name*

AWARDS FOR WRITEGIRL PUBLICATIONS

2015 **Winner**, International Book Awards, Anthology: *Emotional Map of Los Angeles*
2015 **Winner**, National Indie Excellence Awards, Anthology: *Emotional Map of Los Angeles*
2015 **Finalist**, Next Generation Indie Book Awards, Anthology:
     Emotional Map of Los Angeles
2015 **Winner**, Beverly Hills Book Awards, Anthology: *Emotional Map of Los Angeles*
2015 **Runner-Up**, Great Southwest Book Festival, Young Adult:
     Emotional Map of Los Angeles
2015 **Honorable Mention**, Los Angeles Book Festival, Young Adult:
     Emotional Map of Los Angeles
2015 **Finalist**, Foreword Reviews' INDIEFAB Book of the Year Award, Anthologies:
     Emotional Map of Los Angeles
2015 **Finalist**, USA Best Book Awards, Young Adult: Nonfiction:
     Emotional Map of Los Angeles
2015 **Runner-Up**, Southern California Book Festival, Compilations/Anthologies:
     Emotional Map of Los Angeles
2015 **Winner**, Pinnacle Book Achievement Award, Young Adult:
     Emotional Map of Los Angeles
2014 **Honorable Mention**, Hollywood Book Festival: *You Are Here*
2014 **Finalist**, USA Best Book Awards, Compilations/Anthologies: *You Are Here*
2014 **Winner**, The Great Midwest Book Festival, Compilations/Anthologies: *You Are Here*
2014 **Winner**, International Book Awards, Young Adult: *You Are Here*
2014 **Winner**, Beverly Hills Book Awards, Anthologies: *You Are Here*
2014 **Runner-Up**, Great Northwest Book Festival: *You Are Here*
2014 **Runner-Up**, Great Southwest Book Festival: *You Are Here*
2014 **Finalist**, Silver Medal, Next Generation Indie Book Awards: *You Are Here*
2014 **Honorable Mention**, San Francisco Book Festival: *You Are Here*
2014 **Honorable Mention**, Parks Book Festival: *You Are Here*
2014 **Honorable Mention**, New York Book Festival: *You Are Here*
2014 **Honorable Mention**, Los Angeles Book Festival: *You Are Here*
2014 **Honorable Mention**, London Book Festival: *You Are Here*
2013 **Silver Medal**, Independent Publisher Book Awards: *No Character Limit*
2013 **Winner**, IndieReader Discovery Awards, Anthologies: *No Character Limit*
2013 **Honorable Mention**, Eric Hoffer Award, Young Adult: *No Character Limit*
2013 **Bronze**, Foreword Reviews Book of the Year Awards, Anthologies: *No Character Limit*
2013 **Finalist**, International Book Awards, Anthologies: *No Character Limit*
2013 **Finalist**, Next Generation Indie Book Awards, Anthologies: *No Character Limit*
2013 **Honorable Mention**, San Francisco Book Festival, Anthologies: *No Character Limit*
2013 **Honorable Mention**, Paris Book Festival, Anthologies: *No Character Limit*
2013 **Runner-Up**, Great Southwest Book Festival, Anthologies: *No Character Limit*
2012 **Finalist**, Beverly Hills Book Awards, Anthologies: *No Character Limit*

2012 **Winner**, USA Best Book Awards, Anthologies: *No Character Limit*
2012 **Runner-Up**, London Book Festival, Anthologies: *No Character Limit*
2012 **Winner**, Los Angeles Book Festival, Anthologies: *No Character Limit*
2012 **Runner-Up**, Southern California Book Festival, Anthologies:
       No Character Limit
2012 **Honorable Mention**, Eric Hoffer Award, Young Adult: *Intensity*
2012 **Winner**, International Book Awards, Anthologies: Nonfiction: *Intensity*
2012 **Winner**, National Indie Excellence Awards, Anthologies: *Intensity*
2012 **Runner-Up**, San Francisco Book Festival Awards, Anthologies: *Intensity*
2012 **Runner-Up**, Paris Book Festival Awards, Anthologies: *Intensity*
2011 **Finalist**, ForeWord Reviews Book of the Year Awards, Anthologies:
       Intensity
2011 **Honorable Mention**, Los Angeles Book Festival, Anthologies: *Intensity*
2011 **Winner**, London Book Festival Awards, Anthologies: *Intensity*
2011 **Honorable Mention**, New England Book Festival, Anthologies: *Intensity*
2011 **Finalist**, USA Best Book Awards, Anthologies, Nonfiction: *Intensity*
2011 **Winner**, International Book Awards, Anthologies, Nonfiction:
       Beyond Words
2011 **Winner**, National Indie Excellence Awards, Anthologies: *Beyond Words*
2011 **Finalist**, Next Generation Indie Book Awards, Anthologies: *Beyond Words*
2011 **Finalist**, Independent Book Publisher Awards, Anthologies: *Beyond Words*
2010 **Finalist**, ForeWord Reviews Book of the Year Awards, Anthologies:
       Beyond Words
2010 **Winner**, London Book Festival, Anthologies: *Beyond Words*
2010 **Winner**, National Best Book Awards, USA BookNews, Poetry:
       Beyond Words
2010 **First Place**, National Indie Excellence Awards, Anthologies: *Silhouette*
2010 **Winner**, New York Book Festival, Teenage: *Silhouette*
2010 **Winner**, International Book Awards, Anthologies: *Silhouette*
2009 **Winner**, London Book Festival Awards, Anthologies: *Silhouette*
2009 **Finalist**, ForeWord Reviews Book of the Year Awards: *Silhouette*
2009 **Winner**, Los Angeles Book Festival, Nonfiction: *Silhouette*
2009 **Winner**, National Best Book Awards, USA Book News, Anthologies:
       Silhouette
2009 **Silver Medal**, Independent Publisher Book Awards: *Listen to Me*
2009 **Runner-Up**, San Francisco Book Festival, Teenage: *Listen to Me*
2009 **Winner**, National Indie Excellence Awards, Anthologies: *Listen to Me*
2009 **Runner-Up**, New York Book Festival, Teenage: *Listen to Me*
2009 **Finalist**, Next Generation Indie Book Awards: *Listen to Me*
2008 **Finalist**, ForeWord Reviews: *Listen to Me*

2008 **Winner,** London Book Festival Awards, Teenage: *Lines of Velocity*
2008 **Honorable Mention,** New England Books Festival, Anthologies: *Lines of Velocity*
2008 **Grand Prize Winner,** Next Generation Indie Book Awards: *Lines of Velocity*
2008 **Winner,** National Best Book Awards, USA Book News:*Lines of Velocity*
2008 **Silver Medal,** Independent Publisher Awards: *Lines of Velocity*
2008 **Honorable Mention,** New York Festival of Books Awards: *Lines of Velocity*
2007 **Finalist,** ForeWord Magazine: *Lines of Velocity*
2007 **Honorable Mention,** London Book Festival Awards: *Untangled*
2006 **Finalist,** ForeWord Magazine: *Untangled*
2006 **Winner,** National Best Book Awards, USA Book News: *Untangled*
2006 **Notable Mention,** Writers Notes Magazine Book Awards: *Nothing Held Back*
2006 **Honorable Mention,** Independent Publisher Book Awards: *Nothing Held Back*
2005 **Finalist,** Independent Publisher Awards: *Pieces of Me*
2005 **Finalist,** ForeWord Magazine: *Bold Ink*

Write about the things that
need to be heard.

WriteGirl Publications
Los Angeles

SOUND GENERATION: The Resonant Voices of Teen Girls

Publisher & Editor:	Keren Taylor
Associate Editors:	Cindy Collins
	Allison Deegan
	Annlee Ellingson
	Katie Geyer
	Kirsten Giles
	Kelsey O'Brien
	Corinna Schroeder
	Genevieve Scott
	Michelle Chahine Sinno
Book Production Support:	Sofia Aguilar
	Emily Bradford
	Jana Helms
	Reparata Mazzola
	Rachel McLeod Kaminer
	Lindsay Miller
	Elena Perez
	Barbara Stimson
	Bonita Thompson
Art Director:	Keren Taylor
Book & Cover Design:	Sara Apelkvist
Printing:	Chromatic Inc., Los Angeles

ISBN: 978-0-692-88728-8

FIRST EDITION
Printed in the United States of America

Orders, inquiries and correspondence:
WriteGirl Publications
Los Angeles, California
www.writegirl.org
info@writegirl.org
213-253-2655

ACKNOWLEDGEMENTS

We at WriteGirl wish to extend our heartfelt thanks to each and every one of you who contributed so generously to making this wonderful anthology possible.

Two years have passed since the publication of our last anthology and it is with great pride and excitement that we bring you *Sound Generation: The Resonant Voices of Teen Girls*. This spring, our book production team dove into a sea of submissions from our teens (and a few of our alums) that included poetry, prose, songs and excerpts from novels and screenplays. It has been both a labor of love and an honor to read through the hundreds of pages of submissions sent to us via email, snail mail, text, hand delivery and even snapshots of handwritten pieces. Some pieces were quickly scribbled down at one of our monthly Los Angeles workshops while others were labored over during weekly mentor-mentee writing sessions.

We would like to thank our WriteGirl parents. We applaud your efforts to ensure your daughters' participation in our workshops and mentor-mentee sessions and your enthusiastic support at our public readings and special events.

Thank you to all of our WriteGirl volunteers for your passion and dedication. You provide the safe space in which our girls can explore their voices and share their words freely both on the page and with each other.

To our board members, friends and supporters, thank you for helping sustain WriteGirl, year after year. You make it possible for us to expand our programming, network and partnerships.

Thank you to the WriteGirl book production team of editors, proofreaders and production assistants. Your long hours, late nights, attention to detail and generous spirits made this book possible.

Thank you to Sara Apelkvist for once again lending your creative talents to design this book, cover to cover, in a way that honors and celebrates our girls' words and the spirit of WriteGirl.

Finally, a big thank you to every WriteGirl teen writer. Your creativity and profound courage make this anthology sing!

Write so quickly that you have no time to judge.

TABLE OF CONTENTS

1. REFRESH FOR LIKES: TEEN LIFE / IDENTITY

2. I PREFER TO BE CALLED SOPHIE: FRIENDSHIP

3. INDIE-POP RIFFS: INSPIRED BY

4. FURIOUSLY STIRRING THE POT: FOOD

5. MAMA WOULD SING THE BRIDGE: FAMILY

6. YOU'LL BE MAD AT ME FOR WRITING THIS: CHALLENGES

7. INSPIRATION STATION: WRITING EXPERIMENTS

8. CLICK! WRITEGIRL AT THE HUNTINGTON

9. THE SILENCE OF LEE AVENUE: PLACE

10. A FEW SCRATCHES ON THE GROOVES: MUSIC

11. CAN'T BRING MY HEART TO SKIP YOU: LOVE

12. SUIT UP, SPEAK UP, RISE UP: RESIST

13. LULLABY OF AN AWAKENED STORM: NATURE / SCIENCE

14. THE CRUCIFIX AND THE HOLLYWOOD SIGN: LOS ANGELES

15. THIS IS WRITEGIRL

FOREWORD

Senator Holly J. Mitchell was a special guest speaker at the WriteGirl 15th Anniversary Celebration. When she read this letter to her fifteen-year-old-self, we asked if we could include it in our new WriteGirl anthology. Whether you are fifteen or fifty-five, there is advice here for you, about the importance of self-confidence, individualism, boldness and mindfulness, that is at the core of what WriteGirl is all about.

Letter to My Fifteen-Year-Old Self

My dear, dear Holly:

Thinking about you at fifteen years of age and all that lies ahead of you makes me smile. So to succinctly capture all the stuff swirling around in my head that I want to say to you, I'll resort to my Virgo self and make a list! Here we go:

1. I know it's hard being six feet tall and wearing a size twelve shoe. But trust me…it will be OK. Because next fall the entire boys' basketball team will return from summer break taller than you! And in about twenty years, thanks to personal computers, the internet and enlightened shoe manufacturers, you will shop worldwide and own dozens of really hip shoes! And even though it's hard now, one day you'll grow (not literally…you top out at six feet!) to truly appreciate — even VALUE — your height. Because when you walk in the room, everyone knows you've arrived.

2. Don't be afraid!

(a) Your mom NEVER finds your diary! ;)

(b) When David McDonald tries to kiss you, let him. Nobody will care that you kissed a boy. Your reputation will remain stellar.

(c) When Howard University sends you an early acceptance letter in your junior year, GO! Don't let fear stop you. Your Grandma Jewell will go above and beyond to convince you that you shouldn't go — cost, distance, you'll be alone, etc. While she certainly means well, please know that she lived her entire life in fear. It stopped her from experiencing her own full potential, and you don't want to live life that way. Learning to jump and take risks is a skill that takes practice to master. JUST DO IT.

3. **When you lose your mom and dad, you'll be devastated.** It will feel like all the air left your body. That horrible feeling of being all alone in the world will gently pass and you'll remember that they trained you well. You'll learn you were built tough!

4. **You're a bright, confident young woman and there are some things you've already got right!** Your strong work ethic will take you far. People will notice and give you opportunities to soar. It's OK to slack off a bit…you don't have to work EVERY summer and school break. An internship or a study-abroad experience would do you well. Your bohemian style suits you. So don't ever buy a Lacoste shirt or straight skirt! You will find appropriate ways to express your individuality in all settings. Thanks for having the courage early to strut your stuff and be your unique self.

5. **Your love of writing (and gift of gab) will serve you well throughout your career, so don't stop!** Keep writing! You will have the privilege to write laws that govern the most populous state in the nation. You will honor those who came before you and make history on your own.

6. **You will travel, fall in love, get your first tattoo at thirty years and become a mom at thirty-five years.** The friends you have now at fifteen years will still be in your life at fifty years (with the exception of David McDonald!). Your mentor Ruth will help you navigate many a fight with your mom and your rebellious period (it's brief), and stand proudly by your side at ninety years old when you take the oath of office. She and the other wonderful role models in your life will never fail you, ever.

7. **And finally, you will be amazed at how quickly time flies, so enjoy every moment.** And when you celebrate your "quinceañera reverso" in 2015, you will take a moment to reflect on it all and realize, you are perfect just the way you are.

You go, girl!

Fondly,

Your older, wiser self
California State Senator Holly J. Mitchell

INTRODUCTION

Welcome to *Sound Generation: The Resonant Voices of Teen Girls.* This is a book so packed with stories, dreams, emotions and vignettes that you need to savor it, the way you might keep a special photograph on your desk to be able to look at it often, on different days, over time. This book is best read like that, over time. Every page offers a different teen writer, a new perspective, a fresh view on life, love, lunch or Los Angeles.

While this isn't a book about music exactly, many of the teen authors make some connection to music in their writing. Some of the musical references are clear, but others are not at all obvious, so we give you this challenge: See if you can catch all of the references to songs, bands, musicians, instruments, rhythms and sounds throughout the anthology.

The work in this book comes from two years of workshops and gatherings. Some pieces were written in a day, others took months of revision. The writing process is different for every writer.

This is an interactive book. There are quotes on the craft of writing from our community of writers throughout the book, and two chapters, "Inspiration Station" and "Click! WriteGirl at The Huntington," are filled with a variety of writing experiments and advice to help you explore your own creativity and generate your own personal stories, poems, songs or scenes.

The sparkling fountain of inspiration behind WriteGirl is all of the women writers who volunteer to help lead workshops and mentor girls. They are accomplished screenwriters, songwriters, poets, journalists, fiction authors, memoirists, bloggers and more. Their positive and intensely creative energy fuels WriteGirl and keeps this community thriving and growing, year after year. We mourn the loss of two of our members this year: Elise Kroll and Jennah Ferrer-Foronda. Their joy and creative contributions will always be remembered, and are woven into the pages of this book.

There is a deliberate double meaning in the title of this book, *Sound Generation*. These are voices that will resonate in the decades ahead, leading us forward into making sound decisions and taking bold actions. So curl up in a cozy chair, and whether you dive into "Rise Up" or "Soundtrack of My Life" or "Mindful Mashed Potatoes," we are certain you will feel all the different ways these girls remind us to *never underestimate the power of a girl and her pen.*

– Keren Taylor, Executive Director

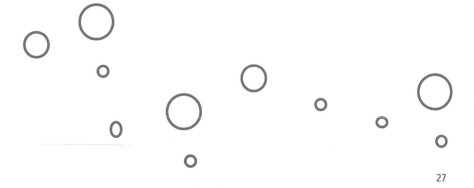

1

Teen Life / Identity

A typical millennial's mental process after posting something.

#summer

I posted a picture of myself
lying down in the sand next to my friend.
We were wearing white bikinis.
Hashtag summer has finally begun!

It's been five seconds and the only person who liked
was my pastor who left the church last year. Hope he's doing well.
It's been one minute now and a girl commented,
fire emoji, heart-eyes emoji, fire emoji.

Compliments, emojis, lies.
Refresh for likes.
Refresh for fulfillment, for enjoyment, for love.
Hashtag bits of dopamine.

I'm waiting.
Hashtag when will my phone buzz.
I receive no notifications.
I Photoshopped this picture to perfection
and there are only 20 likes.
What a shame.

My friend says self-esteem is maximized,
mental health deteriorating.
Hashtag delete.

I wrote this poem last year for the Los Angeles Youth Poet Laureate competition. It was inspired by the problems, ridicule and struggle I've faced through having curly hair over the years but have ultimately accepted as a positive quality.

Curly Hair

A little girl with curly locks, twisted into migraine-inducing braids. Bloody murder from her lips, individuality hidden away, a monster in a sea of straight waves. Tearing at her cursed scalp, she clawed the unruly strands, begging them to straighten. Little girls pet her hair like a petting zoo attraction. Adults fawned over her, exclaimed she was a doll. Doll scalps were straight — she was not a doll but rather an unwanted reject, recalled from toy-store shelves, replaced with a straight blond bun in a dollhouse of replicas. After-school cartoons, straight brown ponytails, braids dragged her head down onto the couch. Magazine covers advertised hot irons in the aisles of department stores. Tiny curious hands, caught red-handed in the bathroom. She dropped her weapon, sentenced to serve time in the corner, mother praising her curly locks.

Vivian Enriquez, age 17

I am not a musical person. When I found out that the theme of the anthology was going to be music, I did not know how I would incorporate it into my poetry. It turns out, writing is one of the only ways I have the ability to be musical. My life experiences and the little research I did on specific instruments inspired this piece.

Trumpet, Harp, Tambourine, Saxophone

When I was born, I was a trumpet.
I shined like clean brass in my father's eyes.
I would feel the vibration of my mother's lips as she sang to me.

Before the age of ten, I was no longer a trumpet.
I was a harp, becoming tired of my parents plucking away
at my innocence each time they yelled.

After mighty percussions
I tried to hide that I was a tambourine.
A tambourine woman with no sign of bruising.

But this is not a sad story.
I am a saxophone.
One that refuses to hide her voice.

This here, this writing, my heart,
the wind that takes a journey through my anatomy,
is how I sound and who I am.

Advice: live life by the ABCs—adventure, bravery, courage.

Don't worry about what people will think of your writing. Write for yourself first.

I listen to music all the time. I love that there is always a song to describe exactly how I am feeling when I can't describe it through my own words. This poem is meant to show the various activities of my life by describing the sounds associated with them.

Soundtrack of My Life

The soundtrack of my life is the clicking of the keys on my computer as I stay up late finishing homework. It is the cheering of crowds at Friday night high school football games and the barking of my dog running to the door to greet me when I come home.

The soundtrack of my life is the wedding band playing "Here Comes the Bride" as I watch my aunt walk down the aisle in her glowing white dress. It is the ringing of my alarm clock at precisely 5:27 every morning and the drip-drops of scattered rain that come every December.

The soundtrack of my life is the clacking of my tap shoes as I do a shuffle, toe-heel. It is the honking of geese on Sengekontacket Pond every summer morning, and it is my best friend and I laughing obnoxiously loud together.

And for all those moments of joyous sound there is a stark opposite. The soundtrack of my life is also the sniffling of my stuffy nose when I get sick. It is the funeral band as they lead the procession out of the church.

Through all of this noise, there is a song to complement every emotion that I am feeling.

And in that, I find solace.

Katarina Lashley, age 17

In this song, I was imagining why people choose to leave their home, or the person they love.

Forgive Me

You look around in the empty town,
and see that I am gone.
By the theatre, by the park,
by the bakery
with its line too long.

I left, and you'll never know what I felt.
You'll just know that I am missing.
I hope someday
you'll forgive me.

We were living the lives that children live,
kids turned to teenagers,
trying to fit in.
I tried to squeeze inside a skin
that wasn't mine.

I tried to find a place to belong.
Turns out, I was in it all along.

I left, and you'll never know what I felt.
You'll just know that I am missing.
I hope someday
you'll forgive me.

18 Lunar Years

The moon tells me stories, stories of
old rituals and ancient times,
its thoughts on life and the world.
The moon knows my story,
all my 18 years of moons, all the different phases.
We've grown together,
starting out new:
dark, stormy,
growing into something
full, transparent.
She lights the night and paves the way for the day.
I hope to embody her light and
bring a path to those in the night.
The moon tells me stories. She reminds
me of the gift that this is, the 18th year,
the pivotal point,
the edge of the cliff,
the brink of what is known.
So tonight, the last night of 17,
I will hold hands with the moon, and together
we will step into the edge of tomorrow.

I wrote this because this is me — the titles of music that have changed me. I started writing this at a WriteGirl workshop at the Huntington, and I feel like I came a long way and learned plenty of things about music that I didn't know before.

My Playlist

I come from singing Doo-Wops and A Cappella,
being my own Dangerous Woman,
strutting and being confident and a Q.U.E.E.N.
Fake Loves and Ill Minds to Blessings I can never forget
to always hold true.
The False Advertisements of Victorious victories.
Traveling and seeing the Vegas Lights shining for miles,
but still being a Cali Girl at heart.
Covering myself with every song of the world,
from centuries to come, and having my L.A. Love.
Fallin' Out and into Misery Business
and finding myself.
Being Just Fine, listening to myself, being myself.
Having some of the Best Mistakes with some Deja Vu along the way,
I'll never Get Around, Without Myself
Being Crazy but also Genius and starting over to Repeat.

I wrote this piece after the very first WriteGirl workshop we had this season. The positivity of the environment and the bright outlook on the status of women really spoke to me, and I wrote this to commemorate how my views were revived.

For Her Liberty

Though the sun's last rays had faded to dusk, the first drops fell anew to seed her truth. Through the cracks of her roof, splintered black-blue, they sprinkled her face, lit by lucid youth. The night was still young when she saw their fires burning stilted echoes through her tears. They cast long shadows that played across her eyes, a stamp of mortality, to which she'd belong. She followed the silhouettes as they beat the same trail they'd trodden a mile's time behind. Followed them even as they were triumphant in their arrogance, prideful of the paths she had paved. They never heard her, never knew her, never looked her way but for those rare moments of contemplation. Yet still, their entitlement served their fall as it did their rise, and as they winked out, ever reluctant, ever sure, as their nights spread thin as their wills, only then did she pen her own tale, sing her own anthem, waltz the rain away.

Three Days

Our Valentine's Day
lasted for three days.

On day one we took
our first salsa class.
We twisted, dipped
and enjoyed our time of peace.

Day two we played
volleyball at Venice Beach.
He served, I spiked,
and neither of us accepted defeat.

Last, we traveled to Paris
and ate dinner in the Eiffel Tower.
Between his hearty laugh and my
twinkling eyes, I realized
he's the love of my life.

Victim Mentality

Verse
Stuck in one state of mind
One look, you think I'm fine
Every day, you've been so rough
Left me with cuts I just can't stitch

Verse
You came into my life unexpectedly
At first I tried to be friendly
But then you drink my dreams
You aren't what you seem

Chorus
You're a home-wrecker
a gold digger
I don't want
your dirty tears on me
Or your victim
mentality

When you write,
remember that you
are a
contributing thinker.

*Tindi joined WriteGirl after moving to the United States from Tanzania.
We asked her to share her poem in both English and Swahili.*

Mimi Ni Mtoto Sina Mama

I Am a Child No Mother

Mimi ni mtoto sina mama	I am a child, no mother
Mimi ninakja kuishi nawewe	I am coming to stay with you
Tafadhali nijari	Please take care of me
Mimi ni mtoto sina mama	I am a child no mother
Nikumbatie kwa upendo	Hug me tight with love
Nibusu kama mama yangu	Kiss me as my mother
Niambie wanipenda	Tell me you love me
Mimi ni mtoto sina mama	I am a child no mother
Tunza afya yangu	Take care of my health
Nilishe chakula kizri	Feed me yummy food
Nipeleke shule	Take me to school
Mimi ni mtoto sina mama	I am a child no mother
Usini nyanyase	Don't abuse me
Usini uze kwa wanaume	Don't sell me to the man
Usini singizie bali unitetee	Don't accuse me, but be my defender
Mimi ni mtoto sina mama	I am a child no mother
Nipende kila siku	Love me everyday
Bila kujali nifanyalo	No matter what I do
Nipenda kutoka chini ya mayo wako	Love me from the bottom of your heart
Sababu mimi ni mtoto sina mama	Cause I am a child no mother

Stacy Lee, age 17

I took my favorite sounds growing up and compiled them into a poem. I value each and every sound of my youth.

Breathe

Inhale ... singing classes with the excitement of being loud for once.
Exhale ... my favorite ABBA songs coming from the radio.
Inhale ... the laughter from my classmates when we played together.
Exhale ... an orchestra at the Walt Disney Concert Hall playing in harmony.
Inhale ... my mom singing a lullaby as she rubs my tummy to make
          it feel better.
Exhale ... music from instruments my sister would play.
I breathe the sounds from my childhood.

The inspiration for this song is a dumb boy.

What It's Like to Be Confused

Verse
You make me feel like I've slept
through the week,
and I didn't even get to see
your face in my dream.

Chorus
This is what it's like to be confused
(what it's like, what it's like).

Verse
You're the ring I dropped
down the drain.
You're the ugly sweater that got
stepped on in the rain.

Chorus
This is what it's like
to be confused.

Verse
I hope you get gum in your hair
and can't get it out.
Forget your pencil while taking a test.
I guess, I maybe love you.

Courtney Hayforth, age 17

During the WriteGirl Poetry Workshop at the Pasadena Public Library, one of the guest poets encouraged us to write about an imperfection we had and turn it into a positive memory.

I Am Not Perfect, but My Imperfections Remind Me of Something That Is

The air cuts across my weathered skin.
Weak and fragile,
it puts up a good fight,
but there were casualties
from this war seen
in the form of dry flakes
leaving my body's surface.

When it's cold,
my skin, a matryoshka doll,
comes off in layers,
but those dead cells
take me back
to thirty-degree weather,
winds strong enough
to whistle in my ear,
the simplest harmonies
to my middle-school
years in that small town,
Fort Mill,
with more trees than cars,
where nature dominated civilization,
where I first met
my best friend.

Appeal to the heart.
Don't just tell a story,
make them feel!

Be honest and courageous in your work. Writers are Truth Tellers.

Band Director

All the band boys and all the band girls fear him.
He is brutally honest.
He will make you bow down to his queen,
the chicken foot.
Pray you don't miss a note.
Or come in a beat too late.
Without Mr. Ellis, we would never be able
to call ourselves anything more
than kids who own an instrument.
Without Mr. Ellis,
we would never be
Musicians.

2

Friendship

I PREFER TO BE CALLED SOPHIE

Taylor Blackwell, age 18

It is important to sometimes turn off the news and enjoy the company of others. This started as a poem and turned into a song.

Don't You Know?

Here, there you are
stretched out on the floor with your arms over your head.
There, here you are.
I'll feed you tea and oranges like Leonard Cohen said.

The wilting black-eyed Susans.
If love's a game we're losing.
I like lilies better, don't you know?

Here, there you stay
bundled up in blankets up to your chin.
There, here you stay.
We'll keep warm while the ice is growing thin.

The polar bears are dying.
Is there love in lying?
Your words kill me, don't you know?

Throw on your Bowie tee.
Go fetch the morning coffee.
We'll read news in drudgery,
the world around us crumbling.

This came from a prompt to write about a gift (any gift, whether it's physical or not) that you have received.

Gifts

Texts, calls and conversations that last from 8 p.m. to 4 a.m. It starts off with a "hello." Then a game of 20 Questions (more like 100 Questions). Then there are pauses in between, that last a minute, or two, or five, usually checking if our parents will catch us and take our phones away for staying up at such an ungodly hour.

After that passes, an "are you okay?" comes into play. Cue 10-20 minutes of mushy, angsty teenagers ranting about mood swings, feelings and crazy, unbelievable events that occurred in their lives. Then the compliments, comfort and praise come in.

Losing track of time, it's now 4 a.m. A goodnight is whispered into the phone or typed. A yawn or two are heard. The possibility of someone already passed out lingers in the air. *I'm looking forward to the same thing tomorrow night.*

Savannah House, age 15

This piece is about two best friends who mean the world to each other. It is written from the perspective of a male, but it is not a romance.

Trees and Books

"Come here," I said, with daring eyes. We had been reading for hours, and I had finished the three half-read books I'd brought to the park.

She looked up from her book, puzzled, and stood up, stretched and smiled off her yawn. I grabbed her book from her hand and put it down on the blanket in the grass.

Taking her hand, we walked four trees behind our makeshift book nook. I looked back at it in the distance and it surprised me. Food sat in pizza boxes and cookie trays, napkins and beat-up old lunch bags. The light pink feathered blanket blended in with the grass and scattered blossoms, fallen from the trees above.

From any other perspective, she was looking at me. But I knew her too well; I knew she was looking past me. She stepped back from my hand and I let it drop to my side. Her silhouette in the sunlight was beautiful.

She smiled for the first time in weeks, and looked me straight in the eyes. "Let's dance," she said.

What can you see, hear, feel, smell?

Always have a blank
book to write in by
your bedside table
for all your
amazing ideas.

I started this piece at one of the WriteGirl fiction workshops. It was inspired by one of the interactions I can remember when I was younger and used to just play outside. I wanted to convey how our perspectives of the world change so intensely as we get older.

Butterflies Are Better

Nudging his overgrown, honey-toned hair behind his ear, Luke impatiently shifted his weight from leg to leg. I stretched out from my crouched position, leaning into a crumbling branch in what we coined as the "stinky tree." Fortunately, the season of uncomfortable heat was fading, along with the unbearable stench of the white blossoms.

At the age of seven, a height and age inferior to Luke, being better at climbing gave me an arrogant confidence, evident in my agile descent from the tree. My pink scrapes were worth the look of guarded envy in his eyes; I knew this admiration was held sullenly. It was blatant in the way he crossed his arms over his chest, pretending to be bored. I swung onto the last branch and jumped onto the dying grass, feeling the landing shock bounce through my knees. Luke rolled his eyes and turned up the soft acoustic Jack Johnson music playing out of my embarrassingly pink Hello Kitty CD player.

We marched across the yellow grass and headed into his garage. He darted into his house, grabbing two packs of cheese and crackers. I settled onto a black camping chair, trying to ignore the stinging of my scrapes. Luke tossed me a pack, enthusiastically explaining to me that this was his favorite snack. It was foreign to me that day, but I bit into the cracker, and the saltiness of not-actually-real-cheese spread inundated my mouth.

I sunk further into the seat, listening to Luke breathlessly speak about the new butterfly net his grandmother got him, and how we should run over to the flowered bush across the street and see if we could catch a couple of the butterflies hovering there. Thing is, we didn't know that they were actually moths.

Valerie Michelle Chavez, age 16

This poem is based on a past friendship that took a dark turn. Back then, I felt as if I was stuck in a cycle and that I had no choice but to stay and see the end of it. When I regained some courage in myself, I was able to make this poem as a sort of anthem, allowing me to break free from that cycle. Chronophobia is a fear of the passing of time. Anamnesis is reminiscence.

The Days You Stole

Give me back the radiance of the clockwork's chime
the harmony of dissonance
the parable of chronophobia
the trinket of wry gears.

Give me back the irony of melancholy
the pet name of smeared pigment
the asymmetric sewn rag doll
the diverted anamnesis.

You, the paperboy of empty newsletters
the reflection of colliding pendulums
the one who spoke of rains that blossomed a spectacle of lights
the puppeteer of drained strings.

I am timelessly allegiant to you but —
give me back the days you stole.

My Best Friend

You're a counselor
and a comedian.
You're a refuge
when it all seems like too much.

I want to say thank you
for the endless phone calls
the multitude of jokes
the wiping of tears.

Knowing I will always love you
even if you drive me insane
because I know I do the same …

Life is about to pull us in different directions
but no matter where we go
I will always find my way back
to your open arms.

Lauren Cook, age 18

I don't know. Friendship is weird.

Friendship

"Hey, I was going to buy that!" the girl snapped at me.

Startled, I jumped back. She had long brown hair, was kind of plump in physique, and had on a plain pink T-shirt that had the logo of this band I was into (at the time, at least). But what I remember most were her emerald green eyes.

"You like Starlight by Midnight?" I said, shocked, slowly dropping the cotton-candy perfume I clutched in my hand onto the floor.

The girl nodded slowly, still scowling. Dang, I thought to myself. Did she want the perfume that badly?

"Yes. Why do you ask?" she said warily.

"It's just that not a lot of people even know that band exists, and their music is kind of my lifeline right now," I gushed happily.

"Wow, you must have a really boring life if you rely on some band to make you happy," she said bluntly. As she walked away, she turned back and said, "Well, at least you have good taste in music. I'm Sophia by the way, but I prefer to be called Sophie."

Still kind of dazed by her approach, I mumbled, "Marissa."

A new friend inspired this song.

I Go Crazy

Verse
Her long brown hair is flowing
Silly tresses ever-growing
By all means her ripped jeans
Make me hazy. I go crazy.

Verse 2
The way she moves is hypnotizing
I just want to keep her smiling
The way her eyes stare at me
I see a deep chocolate sea.

Adre Yusi, age 21 | *Alumna*

My best friend and her strength inspired this piece. I wanted to take the time to show my appreciation and admiration for her through writing this poem. I wrote this while studying abroad in Madrid, Spain, and missing my best friend.

Marilu

Has saltwater in her veins
and skin that everyone wants to kiss,
but she reserves it for the sun.

eyes that twinkle hazel
change with the fire in her soul:

some have tried to put it out.
she burns the attempts but remains loyal light for those she loves.

languages of burdens passed down to her, never resenting their origin,
proudly worn on every conversation she speaks.

heart tougher than when waves crash
because
she
has saltwater in her veins.

Lucy Eller, age 17

My inspiration is summer camp.

I'll Give You a Banana Split Without the Ice Cream, or Peeling the Banana Because Life Is Full of Disappointments (But at Least You Have the Cherry on Top)

Verse
You know that there isn't much that I hate
more than using overused clichés.
But how do you do that voodoo you do
when you do what you do
like there's something to prove.

Pre-chorus
So I get to be some thousand miles away
with memories of you driving me insane.
And we both know I'll see you soon.
But here's what I have to say to you:

Chorus
I'm sorry I couldn't stay,
but you never wanted me anyway.
Sorry that I wasn't enough.
Go ahead, try and call my bluff.
I know your favorite wasn't me,
but mine was always you.

3

Inspired By

INDIE-POP RIFFS

Arielle Davis, age 15

This poem is about celebrating your culture with one word: Pollera, a Spanish term for a traditional long skirt with colorful decorations used in festivals and folklore.

Pollera

In houses on stilts, the people rejoice.
Someone in Panama has died.
No one is sad.
They pay homage and give respect.
This is a family gathering.

I peek from behind the legs of father and see
seven ladies walking down the church aisle
wearing white dresses with red and green bands on the sleeves.
Wire and beads pull their hair taut,
reminding me of swans.
Our cousin's large lips have been smothered with red lipstick.

They are sisters and friends,
my father explains as they dance down the aisle.
It is a time of remembrance and celebration.
The young women are beautiful.
"Daddy, can I have a Pollera?'

I wrote this piece at the first WriteGirl workshop of the year. It was inspired by a photo of a girl in a flowing dress who seemed to be dancing in the night sky. I wrote "Halley" to describe Halley's Comet, which is only visible every 75-76 years, falling to Earth.

Halley

Her dress was of the finest silk, darker than the blackest night. She was lighter than air, dancing in the cloudless night sky.

The planet's gravity drew her near, but she was not to be stopped. She bounded through the galaxy, faster than the speed of light, silent as a whisper. She could feel them calling to her … She would not be deterred.

But they were coming, and she knew it. She knew it like she knew her name. They were coming. She moved faster, unimaginably fast, inexplicably rhythmic. She laughed, not for joy, but with a hunger … a hunger for more speed, more swiftness. Her skin began to heat up, scorching red hot. Earth was calling to her now. She let its gravity take her. She was ready. She let herself go … and she

crashed.

All that could be seen was a ball of pure speed, fiery energy, blinding light, falling to the surface of the water-covered planet.

Taya Kendall, age 16

*I wrote this while meeting one Sunday with my WriteGirl mentor Erin
and she tasked me with writing about my favorite song at the time
(which was "Violet" by Hippo Campus) and how it made me feel.*

Violet

tastes like nectar and honeydew and sugar / a song for all coca-cola
summers / indie-pop riffs, immortalizing "violet, tryna start your
riot" / feels young, like speeding in a cloud of giggles / down a
midnight strip of highway into the midday sun / while sealing
chapstick-kissed love letters in the back seat / straight to malibu,
care of minnesota / reckless and teenage and free and floral and
warm and everything that late may and early june should be /
sunglasses at the beach / baptized by the waves / sun-kissed pretty
lies by the hot ball of radiation in the sky / this town belongs to us /
not to / politicians / society / standards / convention / or any other
clichéd 16-year-old thing to say / it doesn't belong to anybody who
isn't right here in this nancy drew-blue convertible / no idols / no
rules / just violet

I wrote this piece after looking at a sculpture at the Museum of Contemporary Art in Los Angeles by Andrew Lord called Pressing and Squeezing. *The sculpture was of several imperfect clay pots and vases that were still in their molding stages. A little bit of gold was present in each pot and vase.*

kintsugi

I
the gold seeps into the cracks.
i have yet again failed at
pressing out these jagged edges.

pressing and squeezing and trying to change my jagged clay life,
i seem to be porcelain and stuck in this frame.
the gold covers me whole and i am okay for now.

jagged i am, with lumps and bumps
i endlessly try to press and squeeze away.
i take refuge in this lifeless gold.

II
a porcelain doll, i am not.
i am not fragile and
painted with pastel colors.

i am clay.
i swear to god i could change if i tried and
i don't need to be beautiful because i am strong and stable.

there is so much pressure these days
to be and to be and to be.
i will not break. i am clay.

Someone once said, "Mistrust is what can disrupt." I believe deeply in this sentence because without trust, you can't achieve the goodness in life.

Trust

Five letters. One syllable. Various meanings.
The dictionary has a few definitions:
to place confidence in someone;
to be confident;
a duty imposed in faith and confidence.

What is trust?
Is it letting someone pierce your ears?
Or is it much more?

Truth is
without trust,
there would be nothing.

Friendships, relationships, work,
family, societies, nations, governments,
would fall apart.

Next time you say, "I trust you"
make sure that you mean it.
Next time you hear, "I trust you"
realize how greatly this person thinks of you.

Now tell me,
what does trust mean to you?

When I'm faced with a blank page, I force myself to type. Even if it is nonsense, I will eventually find the words I'm searching for.

When I'm facing
a blank page, I try
to write what I am
afraid to say.

*This is a revised version of one of my very first WriteGirl pieces.
I liked the idea of two people living together, but not really.*

Solitary Roommates

At three in the afternoon, Eliza wakes up to unwashed cups
of coffee in the sink and the shower mat still damp. There's a
covered plate in the oven, bacon and eggs gone cold, cooked at
10 a.m. She switches the radio station back to 104.3 and eats her
brunch to pop songs, saccharine-sweet, like angel cake.

She washes the dishes for Valencia, a thank-you for the food, and
opens the window. Fresh air streams in. She still has six hours
before she has to go to work, the graveyard shift at the nearby
B&B. She uses her time wisely, working on college apps.

Valencia offered to help — she is a student herself at a nearby
college. Her parents are rich enough to afford the tuition.
Sometimes Eliza leaves her essays and resumé out on the chipped
wooden coffee table, fishing for input. She always finds them
marked up in purple ink — Valencia deems red ink too harsh on
the eyes — with suggestions and encouraging notes written in
the corner.

At six in the evening, she opens the refrigerator door, finding
their supplies woefully depleted. On the grocery list, Valencia has
already written, in bubbly letters: "more eggs." Eliza adds, "milk,
lettuce, tomatoes." She eats a heavy supper of pork and rice, and
slides a covered plate into the oven for Valencia before going to
take a shower, preparing for work.

Sabrina Youn, age 14

This is mildly based on a conversation I had once. We were talking about traveling or settling down — nonsense like that. I found myself leaning toward "settling" more than my friend. Even in games (aka Minecraft), I tend to find a base or home quickly rather than explore on and on.

When I Go Seeking

Eyes atwitter and pupils large
I grow my wings and spring off
Zealous, I brush them with feathery quills
compensating for my stolen gold jewels

My knees are on fire, my fingers to nails
filled with melodies my brain forever holds
I look and look, every spot in the world
every nook and crack and mouse's abode

The widest of valleys, the steepest of hills
the vastest of seas and the coziest of trees
I dig in the craters made by the stars
I sleep next to orchids in the night of the dark

I trudge and drag, wearily move on
in hopes that one day, I can call my home
But days morph to years like a butterfly's demise
the caterpillar, free and born once again

Dreams fill my mouth, my teeth turns around
I gnash my tongue, spitting out tears
When shall I stop and where can I say
I am finally at peace and this is where I stay?

Lydia Tucker, age 16

My mentor and I had to describe a flower as music.

Orange

The flowers curved like an alto saxophone.
The orange screams out of the picture,
makes you feel as if you're an eerie E note,
vulnerable to emotions.

Katherine Pyne-Jaeger, age 16

This piece is an excerpt from Out From Galilee, *a much lengthier poem in the pantoum structure.*

Out From Galilee (An excerpt)

Felt clouds shift and burst, tectonic plates move,
and said *no, not today* to that apple-peel soldier.
A soft-beaked bird God peering out between ribs
is enough of a home, and too little of a law.

Said *no, not today* to that apple-peel soldier,
sang of blood, sang of tin, what a sea might become:
enough of a home, and too little of a law.
Drown in a trench of angels, cries the water.

Sang of blood, sang of tin, what a sea might become
poured over deserts and white thousand candles.
Drown in a trench of angels, cries the water,
those ministers of grace, rachides of hands.

Poured over deserts and white thousand candles
is the full sun fluttering in shuttered eyes.
Ministers of grace, rachides of hands:
everything is as blue as the first chord of rain.

This is part of a collection of poems inspired by the Greek myths about Zeus's love affairs. The stories always paint the women as victims of their narratives without a voice, so I wanted to reimagine them in a way that empowered them.

Lovers of Zeus: Io

i.
cow-eyed maiden you
soft-lowing mother you
wandering mind you never sleep

ii.
she dons the garb of laborer
toiler in the fields
low back, hips that sway like
mama's music taught her

daybreak cracks the whip high singing
working three shifts for five mouths
she doesn't look back
doesn't suit her

iii.
waiting weighs on the heart like stale musk, silent disguise.
reckoning waits for no man, and why should she? never
made an easy break, always left tracks in her wake

there are different kinds of dark, she knows their names.
the kind that seeps up from the cool deep, the kind that stalks,
grainy like static clogging her throat, the kind that
chases on the sleek tails of dreams — that dark is the worst of all

This piece is the opening to a novel I am writing about monsters and their hunters.

London, 1835

Two figures stepped out of the mist on the cobblestone street. Their cloaks hung motionless, faces shaded by top hats. Eliza stared at them moving soundlessly back and forth on the street. Time seemed to stop, and the silence was like an orchestra during a caesura.

The two figures turned toward the window where she stood. They looked at her and started forward. She watched in horror as they reached the black iron fence and in one jump they cleared it, dropping without so much as a crunch on the grass below.

"Let us in, little girl," one hissed, his voice like broken glass. She could see the bottom of his face, the brim of his hat casting the upper half in shadows. He smiled at her, revealing stained brown teeth. "Invite us in," he continued to rasp. She could see the jagged points of his canines extending just below his lip.

The clock in the hall downstairs chimed once. The warmth and light from the fireplace behind her seemed to seep away, and her hands felt the windowpane turn to ice.

Just relax
and write.

Zöe Gerst, age 16

This poem is inspired by Christmas and Hanukkah.

Weird Gifts

Disembodied skeleton hand to hold jewelry
friendship from school
Fart in a can that farts in different tones
inspiration from nature
Chocolate, chocolate, and more chocolate

Unicorn snot to brighten my face
support from Mom and Dad
Foot massages that my mom didn't want
kindness from my boyfriend
Bill Cipher statue because I need a new back scratcher

Antique

Cautious footsteps creak upon
weathered, wooden floorboards.
Curious eyes scan titles of
dusty, long-forgotten piles of books.
Keen ears capture the ring of
rotary telephones wistfully waiting for a call.

Different dimensions linger at every corner,
spinning with unparalleled possibilities.
and then —

a towering, gold-engraved wardrobe.
I step inside, but the 1970s vintage
fur coats don't transport me.

Amid the sapphire-blue, Marchesa china teacups
and cherry-wood grandfather clocks,
I still can't unlock the door of fantasy.

Trinkets and treasures transcend the ages
from past owners to future buyers,
but the present lingers with
the fleeting magic of the moment.

It's always been my dream to go to a jazz club.

: : :
: : :
: : :
: : :

Jazzy Monologue

They see them as earphones. I see them as a time machine. I put them in and close my eyes.

It's the 1920s — women in beautiful, blinding dresses, bright lips, pinched cheeks, brushstroke-like curls contained in a bob spinning after them. Shiny, black, inch-tall heels swiftly moving at the perfect pace, the rush visible in their faces.

Men in suits, hair slicked and shining like oil paint, leading their girls to a dip at the trumpet solo.

I look around — it's like a painting. The walls are red, velvet even, complementing the dimmed light coming from chandeliers. The floor, streaked with different shades of sweat, adds depth to the dark wood.

Under a vintage, now considered tacky light-up buzzing sign naming the club, is the stage, crowded with handsome men in suits playing various instruments ranging from the mellow tunes of a saxophone to the complexity of the piano notes, surrounding a gorgeous woman in a wonderful gown and a feather intertwined within her curls. Her voice elegant, yet powerful.

Begin where you are.

4

Food

FURIOUSLY STIRRING THE POT

Soul Food

A few cups of rice and a couple grocery bags later,
a table of fragrant dishes sits before my mother and me.
The steam from the rice dances in the air before being extinguished.
The peas illuminate the table with their bright green eyes.
The tofu trembles, sensitive to any disturbance,
and the kettle sings for attention.
I sit there, recipe book absent, hand-in-hand with mother,
relishing how her words turned into a cup of hot, steamy soup.

Bibimbap is a Korean dish that literally means "mixed rice." It is the perfect embodiment of my cultural identity as a Korean American.

Bibimbap

I skip my way to the kitchen,
prancing along with the sizzling of the pan.
I watch each particle of oil waltz across the surface with the
flames
and witness my mom take the cutting board to the pan.
She glides the knife across the slate.
In go the diced spam and kimchi.
She sprinkles red specks into her creation.
In goes the Korean pepper powder.
She folds all the ingredients into the rice
and scoops the bibimbap from the pan to the bowl.
A slice of American cheese is laid on top,
all the ingredients, together and not separate.
I take a bite,
Korean and American,
and I am happy and content.

Addissyn House, age 17

This poem was written about my transition from California State Summer School for the Arts back to school, where there was an extreme lack of creativity and freedom that I had gotten used to over the summer.

Valencia Orange Peels

Orange wedges dribble down my tongue thick with frustration and heavy with chemical equations.

Orange juice sticks to my fingertips as they graze pencils stuffed in a backpack too big, getting lost in dust bunnies, lint, yesterday's failed quiz, clinging to fantastical teenage crushes on summer's dying cheeks.

Orange pulp buries itself under my fingernails because anger commanded me to dig deep. It will stay there all day, a bitter afternoon snack.

Orange peels dry on my lunch tray, the day gone, dreams disappeared and grades lost to the failing calculator hurriedly sprinting a marathon, out of breath.

They don't curl in artful organic compost and mesmerizing words, stacked into lint-free pockets, soaking in creativity, becoming inspiration for tomorrow's hot day.

These aren't Valencia orange peels.

Write something rooted
in a setting you know.

Juliana Fong, age 13

I was inspired by the sensation I felt when I practiced mindfulness.

Mindful Mashed Potatoes

I see darkness,
hear a soft chatter,
smell the scent of rich gravy.

The goal is to focus,
sit with my legs intertwined,
taste the sweet flavors of the meatloaf glaze.

Count breaths,
in, out,
in, out ...
I feel the potatoes start to melt on my tongue,
the meatloaf start to break apart.

I drift away,
to a cherry blossom field,
my mind restless.

I open my eyes and gasp for air,
finally swallow.

I feel calmer,
yet more awake,
ready to snap back
$E=mc^2$.

Hot Chocolate

The mug of hot cocoa
warms my chilled hands.
The fire and blanket
warm my body.

White marshmallows
melt into the brown liquid
like snowflakes on warm dirt.

I lay my head on a pillow
in front of the roaring fireplace.
Grandma comes and sits
in the rocking chair next to me.
She sips her cocoa.

She tells stories of her childhood.
I listen and smile,
thinking about how alike we are.

Isabel Petty, age 14

I wrote this at the WriteGirl Poetry Workshop. My family makes fun of me for smelling my food before I eat it.

Bite

I pick my fork up off my intricately woven placemat.
I feel the metal go from cold to warm under the heat of my hand.
I dig out a piece of homemade apple pie
and my heart skips like a stone over water.

I watch the steam dance,
as if a snake charmer is playing an invisible, silent flute.
I breathe in the comfort of knowing what I'm about to eat.
I can smell the vibrant colors and the rest of my senses perk up like a
meerkat on a rock.
I take a bite, and my whole body feels relaxed and at peace.

Share food together.
Not just text messages.

Sofia Aguilar, age 17

I was inspired by my grandmother and how proud I am to be her granddaughter.

Posole

Like a desert begs for water,
I beg for posole every Christmas.
The spicy decadence and flirty favors
tempt my open lips.

White lights embrace the tree,
presents wrapped in colors I cannot name,
and grandmother furiously stirring the pot.

Smoke, quickly fanning out
like sunlight onto mustard-yellow walls,
meat rising to the bubbling surface.

The scent reaches me
before my feet reach the front door,
I race into my grandmother's house,
my heart leaping.

Nagymama is the Hungarian word for grandmother.
Koszonom means thank you, and Szivesen means willingly.

Hungarian Kitchen

This moment,
between *nagymama*
and her granddaughter.

A wrinkled smile, brown eyes shine
behind old glasses.
"*Koszonom.*"

She coos, oh tiny one.
The little girl whispers, "*Szivesen.*"

Oven beeps.
Tiny giggles.
Flour on the floor.

Pride fills the kitchen,
love overwhelms the heart.

This poem is one in a series of many in which I work to unpack and understand my family's complex history as Salvadoran immigrants.

Cabbage

Mami always hated cabbage —
thought it too sticky, too slimy, too soggy
when boiled then served
bare on the lonely plate.

At the rickety-walled house in Santa Ana,
Mami's family had a head of cabbage for every day
of the week. Sometimes frijoles negros,
a sliver of queso fresco
if God allowed it.

Forty miles and a world away in San Salvador,
Papi loved cabbage best in
sopa de res — the way it swam
in the soup's juice
smelling of cilantro and onion and yucca
while the beef and papa made a life
raft out of its skin.

A forest of fruit trees in his backyard,
the mangos a ripened saffron and the
mamey sapote waiting to be eaten raw
or made into a beverage and sipped loudly.

My family. This is for my mother.

Caldo de Queso

The smell intoxicates my home, traveling from the stuffy kitchen all the way up to my isolated room. The taste, so rich — my taste buds dance to a song that is sacred to my mother.

Serrano peppers cling to the back of my throat, causing me to cough and cry with joy, giving the rich taste a kick — the warmth traveling, settling in my stomach. A hug from a woman I have never met but will always know.

The memory filling my heart, feeling the lives of the people before me, feeling their warmth and love.

Write a page
beginning with
"What if?"

Lydia Tucker, age 16

I was inspired by memories of my grandma and her cooking.

Oxtail Stew

The faint smell of onions and bell pepper makes my skin
tingle and my stomach impatient.
My grandmother makes the gravy,
her eyes squinted and lips tightened,
letting me know I'm about to have my favorite stew.

Once I see the oxtails floating in the brown gravy
with rice peeking out,
I can't stop eating.
My grandmother scolds me for eating too fast,
always murmuring that I'm a real Creole.

A side of me that I wished to get rid of,
now I embrace with all of my love.
Oxtails are the bridge between me and a history not always
remembered.
A piece of meat that was seen as garbage
is now a delicacy.

5

Family

MAMA WOULD SING THE BRIDGE

Angelica Cordova, age 17

*This piece was inspired by my mom and how ABBA's
"Dancing Queen" brings us together.*

What's Our Song?

"It *has* to be ABBA!" I say,
mother-daughter dance-offs,
shoulders rolling, hips swaying and bumping,
the lyrics of "Dancing Queen"
coming out in huffs rather than harmonies.

The kitchen was where we played our usual gig.
(When we were on tour, we performed in the car.)
We sang for the plates and mugs
watching from the open cupboards,
while the dishwasher broke out in applause.

Mama would sing the bridge;
I would hum the instrumental.
We sing at the top of our lungs,
and with a bit of rock music,
everything *will* be fine.

Aleea Evangelista, age 16

I was inspired by my childhood and all of the Saturday nights that my family spent together.

Saturdays

My family gathers together on Saturdays. We gravitate toward the households equipped with karaoke machines. Loud uncles, chatty aunts and eager kids pass around the microphone. We crowd in front of the TV to watch the picturesque backgrounds of exotic places that accompany the lyrics.

My uncles recycle the same set of songs, but I don't mind. English and Tagalog songs are sung, and my family immerses themselves in music. When someone sings a favorite like "Sweet Caroline" by Neil Diamond, everyone screams and dances to the chorus. Singers then compare their singing scores. Although I can sing, I have yet to reach that perfect 100. Each person in our family settles into their comfortable spot and occupies all corners of the house.

My dad never sings. He prefers to play cards quietly with my uncles in the garage's fluorescent light. My mom always stays in the living room. As my dad deals the deck of cards, my mom is always the first to jump up to the microphone. My less musical cousins and my younger sister prefer to start up a game of basketball or tag outside. My other cousins and I comb through the karaoke songbook in search of a current hit within pages of dated songs.

In the thick of it all is my youngest sister, Alanna. Her lack of reading ability never hinders her performances. My microphone-hogging sister tends to interrupt a person's song (especially mine), too impatient to wait for her turn to sing.

But as schedules fill up and relatives return to the Philippines, our Saturday night changes. What used to be a weekly ritual has died down to something reserved for special holidays. Still, if my family catches a sample of "Sweet Caroline," we're tempted to scream the chorus.

Angela He, age 17

I'm a first-generation Chinese American. At home, my family speaks "Chinglish," a combination of Mandarin and English. This often results in mistranslations and misheard thoughts. This poem is a reflection of our language.

What?

the substitute for words
tossed into the Atlantic,
left behind in the cornfields,
buried in maroon eye bags.

"shénme?" is "what?" in Mandarin
is disgust at Hǎinán chicken with cooked hair follicles intact,
is dismay at another toenail clipper set for Christmas.

"shénme?" is every word,
every meaning, every tradition, every fact
I don't understand
about *Lǎobà* and Mama.

"shénme?" is the word we hurl
across our two-story house
with the unlucky door-facing stairs, pipsqueak closets
upside-down shower faucets and newfangled rules *Lǎobà*
dictates on spur.

While neighbors and strangers exchange
"dear," "honey" and "please,"
we scream, plead and warble,
"what?"

Anna Stone, age 17

The inspiration for this poem was my sister.

My Sister, the Cape Blue Water Lily

Purple, though they call her blue,
definite in her very nature,
no one can tell her to be like the rest.
No one can know what she's been through.
It's hidden in her core.

She's tinted by a yellow youth
and a past she can't deny.
Her heart longs for stolen color.
Her veins reach for perfection,
but she already has it.

Lindsey Staub, age 17

My history class discussed the influx of Eastern European immigrants to the United States in the late 1800s. I was interested in how cultures assimilated to American life and influenced American culture today.

The Girl Who Lived Above the Butcher

Home meant the thick and heavy smell of raw beef. The music of my Sunday morning was set to the beat of Papa's sharpened knife pounding against a cutting board. The melody was classical Austrian music that defined Papa's childhood in the streets of Münster. Every time a song hit a crescendo, Papa tore through the meat with gusto. It was like a dance, Papa and his knife. The two of them waltzed to the rhythm.

My home decor consisted of hanging flanks and an assortment of cleavers. My house wasn't a popular trick-or-treat destination on Halloween. No child wanted to be greeted at the door by a man with stained, red hands and a cleaver, even if it was just part of the job and not a scare tactic.

My room sat just above the freezer, which meant the floor was icy and I always wore thick socks. My older brother, Tobias, had a room above the cutting board, which meant his sleep was disrupted by Papa's incessant carving late at night. Tobias was going off to college soon, somewhere in New Jersey. I wondered if he would miss the grassy scent of fresh shipments on Saturday morning.

I am Valentina Bauer, the girl who lived above the butcher. My dark hair snaked down my back in braids when I completed my homework on the countertop above the meat display. Blood never made me nauseous, but vegetarians made me sick. My roots sunk deep into Austrian soil, and my branches sprouted poultry in the spring. I carved my initials into the legs that hung from hooks in the butchery instead of into the red bark of trees.

Being a resident of the local butchery made me feel special. I was the girl who could bring quality steak for school lunch.

Break all the rules,
it's art — your expression
is the end game.

9 p.m. Phone Call

I see the greatest minds of my generation falter.
There is nothing quite like the phone call I received
a little under three months ago:
Uncle David, who is really Great Uncle David
but those few letters remove him much further
than just once.
Uncle David, dementia like my grandfather —
it runs in the family farther than our own feet can carry.
Uncle David, night of the election
Uncle David, holocaust survivor
Uncle David, quote "I never thought I'd see a
man like that in power again"
Uncle David, his voice an accent, tattooed
with survival.

This is an excerpt from a story about a girl who is from a very messed-up family.

June Bug

Close your eyes and picture a master bedroom. Pitch-black paint covers the walls, making you momentarily blind if you shut off the lights. There, sitting in the center of the room, is a large bed with a black headboard and black sheets. And over in the corner is a large black bookshelf with rows and rows of portals that can take you to different dimensions and worlds. What you just imagined is my room. Beautiful, huh?

I entered my lair, sighed and ran my hands through my dark kinky hair. I sat on the edge of the bed and grabbed my phone from the bedside table. As I lay back, I thought, "Which one — Lorde, Melanie Martinez or Marian Hill?" There were so many artists I could listen to at that moment, so many voices. I decided I would go with Melanie Martinez, the girl with the unique voice that sent chills to the listener. As I turned on my music and tuned out to Melanie's melodic voice ringing in my ears, a message appeared on the screen of my phone.

An email. Great. I pressed on the icon, sighing in boredom. There, in my mail, was a message from a no-reply email. I clicked on it, curiosity coming out my pores. The words on the message weren't foreign or new. I had heard them many times from my own mother's mouth.

"He used to call you his June Bug — a cute thing it was," my mother would say when she wasn't going through one of her episodes.

"Miss you, June Bug," was written right across my screen. Who else would know to call me "June Bug" besides my long lost father.

Deborah Shonack, age 16

I wrote this piece during a WriteGirl workshop.
It was inspired by my grandmother's passing.

Life's Melody

A music box, wrapped in tattered paper,
tied with a yellowing string.
My name and address,
in her spidery handwriting.

A little girl stands on top,
a tan safari hat decorating her head.
She holds a note that says,
"Listen to the song."
I turn the handle, the song starts,
the little explorer circling to the music.

I close my eyes,
letting the happy and hopeful flute take over,
letting the memories of the past fill me.
The song turns sad and remorseful, the flute
replaced by a cello and violin.

Wiping away tears, I realize my life will become
the explorer's, full of happiness and hope,
confusion and grief,
and that no matter what happens,
the journey was worth it.

The flute returns, hopeful once more.

Pour your feelings out,
then edit later.

I wrote this about my newborn niece.

Teddy Bear

I know I saved my teddy bear for a reason,
its tufts of hair falling on the bedsheets and its bow out of place.

My mother said to donate it, give it to the local Salvation Army store,
but I was saving it for someone.
I was waiting for someone to hold it tightly in her arms at night,
pass it around to her classmates for show-and-tell,
hide it in her backpack for day camp (even though toys aren't allowed).

And now you're here.
I never knew I was capable of loving someone so much.
I cannot wait for the day that we can walk around the block together,
laughing while we sing the next big Disney hit with Teddy in hand.
But for now, I'll let you sleep.

They say dimples are lucky to have.

Dimples

"Where do my dimples come from?"
I asked my mom.
"From your father," she said.
And suddenly I feel so lucky —
I feel like an angel.

I wrote this piece for my father who passed away a couple of weeks before the WriteGirl Songwriting Workshop.

Song to My Father

Verse 1
Father, you slipped away so soon
I promise that I'm not mad at you

Chorus
So, Father, watch from above
I'll always be your little girl

Verse 2
I'll fulfill my dreams as you wanted me to
Do things the world didn't expect me to do

Chorus
So, Father, watch from above
I'll always be your little girl

Creativity has no true rules, but if there are any, you decide them.

Write everything and then rearrange it to be something different.

Bobe means grandmother in Yiddish.
Popo means grandmother in Cantonese.

They Say You've Seen This Before

Dear Bobe,
They say you've seen this before
on the playground when boys
would pull your hair and say,
"Rudoph, you can't play."

Dear Bobe,
They say you've seen this before
when your brothers and sisters cried
and allies turned blind eyes.

Dear Popo,
They say you've seen this before
when you, 18, knew welcome for the first time
and when your children cover their eyes in shame.

Dear Popo,
They say you've seen this before
when your brothers and sisters cried
and allies turned blind eyes.

Dear Grandmother,
They say you've seen this before.
I promise
my children will never see it again.

Mother's Kitchen

Sitting on the front porch
with random thoughts,
enjoying the sunlight
on a Sunday afternoon.

"Scarborough Fair"
playing on the radio.
The smell of cookies
in the oven.

The odor of old bookstores
filled to the brim with literature.
The paper, soft and worn
beneath fingertips.

Sitting on the bench,
waves crashing
on the shore.

The taste of a
red velvet cupcake
when it first
touches your tongue.

A mother's hug,
holding you
just tight enough.

Denielle Mancera, age 15

In honor of my grandmother who passed away recently.

The Mendoza Houses

237th Street,
lucky to have two of the many Mendoza homes —
the brownish pink house
with at least five cars always parked outside,
scooters scattered across the grass,
a single stuffed animal lying on the roof.
The door is always locked; someone is always inside:
Rafael, Michelle, Mark, Frankie, Dustin, Lupita, April
and the baby six-foot-small John —
all eight Mendoza kids, plus Rafael and Felicitas, that makes ten.
Add thirteen more kids to the now-grown eight:
Ralphie, Miranda, Matt, Aaron, Frankie, Denielle, Katie,
Josh, Bella, Chloe, Carson, Riley,
plus the new members Toni, Nicolas and Cookie —
there's always more to come.
Can't forget the husbands and wives: Ellie, Carrie, Gris, Leti Jr,
Shannon.
If you don't find them there,
five houses down there's a yellow house —
that's one of the many Mendoza houses too.

6

Challenges

YOU'LL BE MAD AT ME FOR WRITING THIS

Lena McElroy, age 18

On my second to last day of high school, some kids wanted me to dance in front of other kids in an auditorium. I was too nervous to do it, and they got mad. Later that day, I realized something about what it means to be cool.

Real Cool

I want to be popular. And cool.

But so what? I am not the only one who fantasizes about being looked up to and famous. When I started high school (and even when I was in middle school), I wanted to be "cool." Since then, I've done a lot. I went to an art club, Christian club, Black Student Union, Red Cross club and Interact club. I was on the school's basketball team for three years. My senior year, a lot of people knew who I was. Even people who I didn't know talked to me. I started to feel like someone.

But if you don't do what everyone else is doing, people often get mad at you. It's like you have to please everyone. Popularity is often measured by the way a person dresses, whom they know, whom they date. People mix that up with being "cool." Even I used to do that.

Being cool is being able to accept yourself, even after things don't go your way. Being cool is wanting to be your own person and not letting anyone change you. Maybe I am popular. Maybe I'll be famous. But I think I have a long way to go before I'm cool. The only way I will be is if I say, "World, this is who I am, take it or leave it."

I wrote this for a friend who lives in Utah.

Apart

740 miles apart
I keep you close in quotes and little scraps of paper
I collect you around my heart as you scatter to build a hard shell
I take your hobbies and I fashion them into a sort of crutch

31 days apart
I keep you fresh in promises and jokes at your expense
I write you letters that take too long to get shoved in an envelope
I know already that you'll be mad at me for writing this

14 years together
You running at life with your boxing gloves raised
You taking on mountains because you could
You having years of passion behind minutes of planning

5 minutes staring at the page
I just miss you
I miss you a lot
I start to write

Nyah Toomes, age 16

Every night before I sleep I look at the picture of my grandma and me on the wall. She passed away in 2013.

3:28 in the Morning

Sinking into my bed in a dimly lit room,
a nectar tint takes over the air,
filling the ceiling with its warm color,
crowding my mind.

Alone with my thoughts of you,
no city lights to distract my eyes.
Instead they roam over your picture on the wall,
over and over.

I won't break my stare until my eyes can no longer stay open without effort.
Your memory is burned into my brain.

It's 3:28 in the morning.
I can finally close my eyes.

Anna Stone, age 17

This song is about my struggle to separate my life from the chaos of the mood swings.

Betraying the Carnival

My mind is a carnival,
all the sounds and the lights.
My mind is at war,
all the fears and the fights.
They say it's killing me,
and I know they're right.
But the carnival wants me back.
But the carnival wants me back.

This is my life not yours.
This is my choice not yours.
I'm taking it back
and closing the door.
I'm starting anew.
You can leave the floor.
Because I'm not in the carnival
anymore.

*This is about a girl traumatized by the death of her
sister to the point where she refuses to speak.*

Existence Within a Periphery

After I lost her, I couldn't bring myself to speak again. Like the waves that
break before me, words roll through my mind, never reaching my tongue,
constantly at the brink of surfacing.

The ocean is one of the few things that is constant in my life. Forever blue,
it will always be where my head is clearest, and it won't ever feel the need
to up and leave me, or to die and disappear.

Today, I decided to go barefoot. I feel the sand beneath me and swipe a
few stray grains from my jeans. As I stare at myself in a piece of sea glass,
I see sun-kissed strands of hair that frame my face in a wild, chaotic heap,
and light blue eyes rimmed red and filled with anger. I see caramel-colored
skin so imperfect it's tough to look at.

A wide blue sea lives in front of me and a large, bitter world surrounds
me, but mostly I notice my tears. Today, they're big and fat, slowly rolling
down my face. These are the best kind of tears. They're not sobs, but they
aren't sniffles. They're very wet and they build up in my eyes until my
sockets can't hold them any longer and then spill over.

Don't be freaked out. Make yourself into a character if you need to and be who you wish you could be.

If you're having issues with procrastination, get the belt from a terry cloth bathrobe, wrap it around your waist and the back of your chair, and double knot. if you can't get up from the chair, you can't do anything but write!

This song was written during the WriteGirl Songwriting Workshop. I was inspired by the metaphor of a game where two "players" — two people in a troubled relationship — always end up in a draw in every match.

Warning Signs

Verse 1
That's no way to talk to me, that's no way to greet me at all.
That's no way to compete. If I were you I'd just admit you're at fault.

Pre-chorus
You can play the game if you play it fair.
You can cross your fingers but the luck's not there.
If you stand between me and the finish line
there's a coin to flip and it's surely not mine.

Chorus
No one's gonna call a tie when I deserve to own what's mine.
That trophy is a warning sign. Dare to take your bet or roll the dice.
You're a rookie. Listen carefully,
I've got the cards all stacked up for me.

Verse 2
Don't worry, we're not keeping score,
but if I were you, I wouldn't take a step out your front door.

Pre-chorus
You can play the game but it's rigged for me.
It's a risk predetermined, not a lottery.
Here's your cue to step out of the hazard zone:
I'm up on top and I can't be overthrown.

Chorus
No one's gonna call a tie when I deserve to own what's mine.
That trophy is a warning sign. Dare to take your bet or roll the dice.
You're a rookie. Listen carefully,
I've got the cards all stacked up for me.

Stitches

"Get me the paper towels."

Sam raced across the kitchen and returned in seconds, shoving them into my face. I pressed them against Liam's wound until they were wilted in my hands. Finally, the blood stopped and I carefully peeled back the paper to reveal the wound underneath. My throat dried up. An angry red gash cut across the side of his abdomen where the monster had gotten him. I swallowed back my freak-out and commanded Sam to bring me a wet washcloth. I dabbed it lightly across the wound, disinfecting, careful not to damage it more.

"Hand me the needle," I said, not allowing myself to think or worry.

Sam handed it to me and I grasped the cold metal. My hand shook, tearing a small hole in Liam's skin. I closed my eyes. What did I think I was doing? I'd never been good at sewing. Every time my mother had tried to teach me, I ended up botching the whole thing. Prairie-girl dolls turned into Frankenstein dolls, shirts turned into jagged blankets, breathing boys into not breathing boys.

My heart beat furiously in my chest, like a fist trying to punch through. I focused all my attention on its thunderous pounding. It soothed me enough to be able to open my eyes and start again. I plunged the needle into his side. The stitches were jagged and not at all pretty, but they had to work. It was going to be a long night.

Nina Collier, age 17

I wrote this when I began to realize it was a much healthier path to let go of my negativity and "stop drowning."

I Float

The shore shrinks,
too far to stop now
lungs burning, eyes stinging, legs kicking, stomach churning.
The sparkling ocean winks at me with a promise.
I am inundated with the pressure of this current,
exhausted but carry on
with the rhythm of each wave.
The beaming sun is scorching yet calming.
The organized chaos of this unruly energy comforts me.
I stop struggling
and
I float.

Moon Lit Sonata

The conductor taps his marble podium
and signals the beginning of the impromptu

Moon Lit Sonata. Evident as
her fingers chased the shadows away,
she played until her tips were numb and bleeding,
her grief tangible in every note,
coloring the white keys with her sorrow,
leaving a trail of smudged scarlet and dead dandelions.
The moon above the window's molded frame
covered the room in peaceful gray.

She played as her friend's laugh disappeared from the room,
as the roots of the earth buried his coffin between narrow walls,
as the dead dandelions rebloomed over his grave.
The girl wept into the sheet music.
What she found there lies between the
indistinguishable scent of grief and loss.

Sparkling

I bought a record that felt like a house
because lately ours has been tumbling down

and it feels like,
every time I turn around
you're not there, not there

and it feels like
maybe
you only want me
sparkling, sparkling

but do you remember
dancing on butterfly wings
in the sun hot days
we both burned amber

but when the light turns gray
you can see the hard lines of my face
and you turn away

and maybe that's all I've ever been
maybe all I'll ever be
well, all I'll ever be, to you

A sarcastic look at what people tell others.

Others Have It Worse

"Oh, stop complaining.
This life of yours is easy."

"Stop being so selfish.
Eagles are going extinct,
half the world is dying, and
everyone has it hard."

"How could you be depressed?"

"We put a roof over your head.
Vermont Teddy Bears line your room."

"Look at the bright side. I don't care
if you have a mental illness.
Time to suck it up."

"Really, you're making a big deal
out of nothing."

"You should be thankful that you
have it better than everyone else."

"A kid in Africa has no food."

Forget "write what you know." Write what you're curious about!

Inspiration Station

· · · · ·

Writing Experiments

It's your turn to write!

Find a cozy chair, get a pen and whatever paper you can find. (You can use an envelope, cardboard or even a flyer from your stack of mail!) The next two chapters are filled with writing "experiments" to give you a chance to play with your words and ideas and discover the power of your own voice. Have fun!

Experiment #1

The Making of "You":

We are a diverse culture, from family traditions to geography to what makes our neighborhood unique. It's been said that "it's not where you come from, it's where you belong." Describe one aspect of your culture, whether it is a special food you enjoy with your family, or a place that is special to you. Write about the sounds or scents or textures.

Turn It Up:

Dive into one aspect of what you just wrote about. Do an internet search of the word or object — learn more about its history or origins and see where that takes you.

Max Volume:

Turn back time. Think of a different place — one you visited when you were younger. Write about the place and why you might want to go back there.

After writing this, I feel like I have a better sense of identity.

Where I'm From

I am from a small house on a hill,
from howling coyotes at night or in the early morning.
I am from riding bikes around a cul-de-sac,
all the way up to the grass meadow.

I am from divorce and separation,
from one family to two.
I am from an apartment in Studio City
to a house in Sherman Oaks.
I am from a small town called Monrovia
and from "You don't know what you have until it's gone."

I am from lots of driving
and from the epicenter, known as Ventura Boulevard.
I am from Mel's Diner with my favorite waitress April,
amidst a city bursting with memories.
I am from my grandparents' house in Lynbrook, New York,
from the bright orange rug in their living room.

I am from a small town removed from all the chaos,
from one main street with Library Park and frozen yogurt.
I am from a street fair every Friday night
and fresh-squeezed orange juice in the morning.
I am from a small house on a hill,
holding onto my stuffed bear for dear life.

Color My World:

There is a strong link between color and emotion. In art, color can represent the truth of an object, like an orange carrot, but it can also affect how the viewer feels about the work. Write about a color that you enjoy in your home, in your closet, or in your neighborhood. Write the story behind that color, from your perspective.

Turn It Up:

Pick a color. Write about how it makes you feel in vivid language. Does purple seem majestic? Is yellow like running barefoot in the sand? Is blue your color for honesty? Red can be warm and friendly or evoke anger. Now look around you. What is the first color that catches your eye? Write about why you think it grabbed you.

Max Volume:

Mix up your senses and describe your favorite color to someone who cannot see. Is brown the smell of old books in a library? What does the color taste like? How does it smell? What sound does your color make? How might it feel to the touch?

An ode to the color red and its importance and symbolism
in both classical literature and a female's life today.

O Crimson Red

There she stands.
A veil of crystal beads
clouds her efflorescence of merlot,
like a noble scarlet letter:
O Crimson Red.

As you curl yourself across the brick wall,
ruby roses will eclipse your roots,
and sweet blush will howl from the hollows of your cheeks:
you are but a single shade in the definition of beauty.

O Crimson Red.
As you sit within the concave hollows,
the gift of wine-colored crystal states your value,
your real reflection on paper:
meteors will burn bright with fire.
The mahogany woods are crushed into concrete floors,
but your red bleeds into the moon.

The Creative Process

*Brooklyn-born **Reparata Mazzola** is a published author, a produced screenwriter and an Emmy-nominated writer/producer. As a member of Barry Manilow's backup trio Lady Flash, she recorded seven of his albums and two TV specials and toured the world. She just finished writing the book for two musicals and has two films in development.*

I started out writing for TV talk shows and news in New York. It taught me how to be judicious with words. I moved to L.A. and was approached to write a book, which I adapted into a screenplay. Now I write stories that require lots of research and I love that part of it.

I like to write in my own home office with a cat on the chair next to me. I have to wash all the dishes in the sink and put things away before I can write. At the same time, I'm thinking and organizing my thoughts.

Something to try:

My mentee and I wrote a poem where, for a week, we wrote down everything we observed at five in the afternoon. It was inspired by a García Lorca poem.

Advice for writers:

Get the proper nutrition in your diet.

Take notes from people you respect and then use them as you see fit.

Rachel McLeod Kaminer grew up in the Appalachian Mountains. Her book of poetry As in the Dark, Descend *was published with Writ Large Press in 2016. Excerpts from her current project,* Attendance, *appear at Cultural Weekly. Rachel lives and works in Los Angeles.*

I feel like writing is a way to listen to the world. I also like creating something that makes an experience for a reader.

I take notes on everything around me! Anything that catches my ear or eye. Sometimes a new piece arrives right away, but most of the time I sit down with my notes when I'm ready to write and find lines I want to use or recombine.

To overcome writer's block:

Take notes, write lists, write on napkins…or in notes on your phone. Listen to friends or other writers read aloud. Walk on a new street or take a different route to work.

Advice for writers:

Write for your ideal readers — the ones who really want to hear what you say — the ones who don't judge your passions and your weird interests and forbidden thoughts.

Deadlines are kind of great. When I'm writing with a partner, we meet every week and exchange work (and also snacks).

Find the Song in Your Heart:

At WriteGirl, we say we write songs when words alone are not enough. The song on the following page has a strong message, and even more importantly, it stirs up powerful emotions. It's time for you to express your passions. Write the chorus of a song that expresses how you feel, right now, at this moment. Use a rhyming pattern and tap a beat as you write to encourage a specific rhythm to emerge.

Turn It Up:

Maybe you want to protest injustice, protect our environment or celebrate a friendship worth fighting for. Raising your voice inspires others to join you. It might sound corny, but that's how you change the world!

Max Volume:

Create a slogan for a poster, as if you were going on a march. Now use that slogan as the title for your song. Be sure to repeat the title in the chorus of your song — repetition is a key element of writing lyrics.

*This song was about feeling afraid to step out in life,
yet at the same time I feel empowered to fulfill my
singing and songwriting dreams.*

On the Edge

Verse
On the edge of something better
can't hold back from the light
want to reach for something greater
being out there seems bright.

Pre-chorus
If I told you I was ready
would you help me get there?
Like a dream I've always heard of
could've sworn it was surreal.

Chorus
It's time to make a breakthrough
and let them see me.
No one is holding me back.
This is my destiny.
I'm on the edge
 the edge.
I'm on the edge
of something better.
I'm on the edge
 the edge.
I'm on the edge
of something better.

Verse
Can I get a taste of sunlight?
oh show me what it's like.
They tell me to be patient.
They don't know what's inside.

Pre-chorus
If I told you I was ready,
would you help me get there?
Like a dream I've always heard of,
could've sworn it was surreal.

Chorus
It's time to make a breakthrough
and let them see me.
No one is holding me back
to be who I wanna be.
I'm on the edge
 the edge.

I'm on the edge
of something better.
I'm on the edge
 the edge.
I'm on the edge
of something better.

Bridge
Tell me it will be alright.
Take my hand and we'll go far.
Close your eyes, see the world
from my side.
Don't be afraid, no I can't do this
on my own.

Pre-chorus
'Cause if I told you I was ready,
would you help me get there?
Like a dream I've always heard of,
could've sworn it was surreal.

Chorus
So it's time to make a
breakthrough
and let them see me.
No one's gonna hold me back.
This is my destiny.
I'm on the edge
the edge.
I'm on the edge
of something better.
I'm on the edge
the edge.
I'm on the edge
of something better.

Outro
Tell me it will be alright.
Take my hand and we'll go far
(far).

Collecting Inspiration:

A poem can come from anywhere, but sometimes you need a little help to get started. Find a piece of art, a photograph or a postcard. Take some time to look at all the details, and write a poem that tells the story of what happened before the photo was taken, before the image was created.

Turn It Up:

Try making a list of items that are related somehow — maybe you can find them in one place, or maybe they belong to a special person. You can browse bookshelves, kitchen cupboards or your closet for inspiration. Once you have a list of items, create short descriptions that feature vivid personal details and throw in a few metaphors.

Max Volume:

To make your piece even stronger, enhance the descriptions with specific details that only you can see.

I was sitting in a room with old picture frames all over the walls, wondering the context behind the photographs — the century, the people in them, the truth behind them and if anyone would recognize them. From there, I made a list of related words (images, gold, luxuriant, beautiful, memories, time, tomorrow, today, breaths, music, truth, love, confidence, you). Then I took the missing pieces and imagined some of the stories behind the pictures. This is one of the poems I wrote that day.

Time As You

The image I have of you is rain as time
Luxuriant, precious.
Broken fragments between folds
Tell golden stories
Stories, the lines on your hands cannot
Tell you the truth
My dear, time as you is beautiful
And you *are* time
Finding the seconds in the day
Is like finding the breaths you breathe
And holding on to them a little tighter
You are beautiful
Your heart
The syllabus you speak
Your minutes in beats
The antique laughter of your grandmother in you
My dear, you are beautiful
The portrait of peculiar music
That only you can taste and feel in your lungs
As you harmonize to silence
You are beautiful
If your words were colors in rain drops
God would not recognize the beauty it has had on you
You would be as time luxuriant and precious.

WriteGirl Intern

Lizeth is studying English and Computer Science at Santiago Canyon College. She is hoping to write and animate for production companies as well as become an established author.

The Creative Process

Advice from the WriteGirl Community of Mentors

Jamie Pachino is an award-winning writer for theater, film and TV. Her plays have been published, produced in four countries and honored more than two dozen times. She has written film features for DreamWorks, Disney and Lionsgate; TV movies for Amazon, Hallmark Hall of Fame, Lifetime and more; and written for series television on NBC, AMC, TNT and USA.

I write to find out what I don't know about the world.

Mine was a roundabout way to where I am. I started as an actor, wrote plays, then wrote features and TV movies and now write for series television (while continuing to write plays and TV movies on hiatuses). The only advice I have as a result is: your path is your path. Don't look at others' ways of arriving and think about what you "should" be doing or if they're "better" or "worse" than you are. For me, my goal was always to be a working artist. HOW I made that work was my own journey. If I measured it against how anyone else got to where they are, it would be comparing apples and oranges.

To overcome writer's block:

Write. Write a lot. Write no matter how bad it is. Try very hard not to care. Keep going. Write some more bad stuff. Get to something, anything that has a kernel of truth in it. Throw the other stuff out and start there. Write some more. Rinse, repeat.

Advice for writers:

Learn about ANYTHING ELSE BESIDES WRITING. Travel. Talk to strangers. Learn about other lives besides your own. Fall in love. Get your heart broken. Have experiences. Reach out to others. The more you know about the world, the more you can portray in your work.

Kelley Turk is a screenwriter who has worked on such shows as 7th Heaven *and* The Secret Life of the American Teenager. *She also wrote a tie-in book called* The Secret Diary of Ashley Juergens *and is currently developing a women of history series, with the first season focusing on Marie Antoinette.*

I gave myself permission to call myself a writer after finishing my first script. It was hard work, but I still wanted to write. That's when I knew I had found my career path.

I always read my scripts out loud. It's amazing the things you notice when you do that. There's a rhythm that presents itself that for some reason doesn't come through just by reading it.

The blank page can be a very scary thing. But writing is rewriting, and since you can't rewrite a blank page, you have to fill it. Everything I've ever written has been the result of draft after draft after draft. You always have to wade through the muck to get to the good stuff.

To overcome writer's block:

Give yourself a pass to fill that blank page with imperfect things because that's the only way to get to that final draft.

Advice for writers:

Writers have to have experiences. This includes reading, getting outside, interacting with a variety of people, listening to opinions that are different from yours and opening yourself up to learning the hard lessons. Some of my best work has been mined from the toughest moments of my life.

Read as much as you can. If you find some writing you love, break it down and figure out what you like about it. Write every day in order to zero in on what your voice is and what you want your writing to say.

The Struggle Is Real:

Many writers struggle when faced with a blank page. But your pen will fly across the page when you write about things that lift your emotions. Write a poem about something you love to do — it could be a sport, a hobby, a Sunday morning routine. Tell us about why you love that activity — give us all the details.

Turn It Up:

If you struggle when you begin writing, you can write your own unique poem about the struggle of writing. If writing comes more easily to you, then write about why, when or where you write, and what it feels like.

Max Volume:

Instead of a poem or prose, write a two-person dialogue where your main character loves to write and is convincing a reluctant writer to try it.

I Write

I write because inside my head are worlds,
alternate realities that want to be realized
to fly out into the world
like the demons of Pandora's box.

There are stories in my heart,
moments in life,
too good not to share.
People I want
to introduce to everyone,
places I want others to see.

They whirl my thoughts, cloud my sight
and shout at their chains,
"Let me free."

I write because I want to write,
because I want to share,
because there are stories
out there.

A Recipe for Writing:

Do you ever wish you knew a recipe to make happiness... or confidence? What about a recipe for avoiding drama or recovering from depression? Do you ever wish you could explain an unfamiliar feeling? Some things are just so complicated! Think about a time when your feelings changed. Maybe you were lonely and then became calm; perhaps you were excited, then became frustrated. What were some of the steps that made that transition happen? Write a recipe poem that describes the steps for moving from one emotion into another emotion.

Turn It Up:

A recipe poem can help you write about absolutely anything by imagining different steps and ingredients. This poet borrows the language of recipes to write about her topic in a fresh way. Try writing a recipe for yourself — or for someone you care about who needs some help or advice.

Max Volume:

Imagine a scene in a musical where your main character is just about to sing your recipe. What are the two characters talking about? Write the dialogue that precedes your "recipe song."

I was at a WriteGirl workshop in a library, and my mentor and I were given instructions to go to the medical books and write a prescription for change. I wanted it to look like a real recipe, and she encouraged me to write it.

A Recipe for Change

- Step one is to have a mind like a pot, filled to the brim with ideas.

- Next, take the most fitting thought and toss it into a cup with a splash of inspiration.

- Grab all the pills of outsider opinions you may have, smash them together and throw the ashes away (for they will not be necessary).

- Add a few pinches of salt and pepper, your trusty supporters (who may only be a pen and paper).

- Grasp the spoon of infinity to mix your potion so it will last.

- Drink the brew, really chug it down, and in a flash, you will have the world before you, and it will be yours to change.

Courtney Turk is a television writer who has worked on 7th Heaven *and* The Secret Life of the American Teenager. *She is currently developing a women of history project with the first season focusing on Marie Antoinette. She has been with WriteGirl for two seasons as a weekly and monthly mentor.*

I knew in high school I wanted to be a writer. I think anyone who loves to write has permission to call herself a writer.

I write because I find it to be the most creative form of communication. Words matter. They help us engage and connect and take us to places that only our imagination can allow us to go.

Something to try:

I came up with an activity on writing character descriptions with my weekly WriteGirl mentee that I really enjoyed. We went to a place where we knew a lot of people would be. We each then selected a person to write a description about. But we were not allowed to include their clothes or hair. People often use those as a crutch, and we wanted to really dig deep and think more outside the box than that. We would then swap our descriptions and try to pick whom the other person had been writing about.

Advice for writers:

Embrace criticism. It doesn't always feel like it, but it only makes your writing better. Writing is rewriting. The more you mold it, the more it comes out how you envisioned it.

Read books. It helps open up your creativity and evolve it.

Maiya Williams *was the first black woman elected to the* Harvard Lampoon. *As a TV writer-producer she has worked on such shows as* The Fresh Prince of Bel-Air, Mad TV *and* Futurama. *She is also a novelist of middle-grade books.*

I write best in the morning. Every day I wake up at six, walk the dogs, get my son off to school, eat breakfast and read the newspaper, and then by 8:30 I start writing. I write until lunchtime, then after lunch I continue writing until about four. I don't wait for inspiration, because to me that equals procrastination. But generally I am inspired by strong energy and emotion, whoever it comes from, but often it comes from people in my family. Excitement, happiness, sadness, love, hate — if it's a strong emotion, it excites my mind.

I use a laptop computer and sometimes I have to change where I sit in the house to get the right "vibe" before I can write. I rotate to a new place in the house if the old place becomes "stale."

To overcome writer's block:

Sometimes fresh air, a nice hike or bike ride, or walking my dogs will clear my head. But sometimes the problem is that there is something false embedded in the manuscript, and it takes more digging to find the problem and fix it. That's harder obviously, but feels great when you finally find the problem and address it.

Advice for writers:

Get a good book about the basics of writing whatever form you want to write in, read it, and then write, write, write!

Open yourself up to as many different kinds of experiences as possible because you never know when you can use it in your writing.

Don't criticize your work by coming to the conclusion that you are terrible just because your first efforts aren't great. Believe that you can always improve and be willing to work at it, the same way an athlete works at improving her game.

Playing with Pattern:

Take a closer look at the poem on the following page; do you notice any patterns? Yes, the important words within each line all start with the same letter. Create a poem that uses a pattern of your own creation. You could use a specific number of words or syllables on each line, or you could use a different vowel sound on each line — play with a few pattern ideas until you find one that inspires you.

Turn It Up:

Hide your pattern. Rearrange your lines, or write a different version of your poem that disguises your "device" or pattern. Sometimes just the constraint of a specific "rule" is all you needed to find yourself writing something you didn't even know you needed to say.

Max Volume:

Make this experiment more challenging by adding more patterns and including a color, a gemstone or a name (people or places) in every line.

River

Take thoughts and turn them to me.
I will ingest illnesses and idolize ipecac,
stripping shelves of shirked stories,
coming clean, touching cheeks.

Nicking, noting nigh darkness:
"Once overworking overcomes,
death doesn't seem daunting."
Killjoy, killjoy, killjoy.

Bronze bones buried in bleach.
Lozenges littering lonely streets,
succumbing to slow sorrows.
Reality revamps human rights.

Unfazed, universes continue unwinding us.
Awful, ain't it? Arrogance appears.
Glaciers grow gaping maws, glitzy glitzy.
Thrones of topaz, twinkly tequila, through and through.

8

WriteGirl at
The Huntington

CLICK!

CLICK! WriteGirl at The Huntington

CLICK! WriteGirl at The Huntington Library, Art Collection and Botanical Gardens in San Marino, California, was a series of five summer WriteGirl workshops that combined creative writing, photography and nature. The goal was to help teens establish a connection between the use of smartphone cameras and the creative writing process and to explore how different forms of expression can inform each other.

The Huntington grounds cover 120 acres and offer a dozen gardens for exploration, making it an ideal setting to experiment with photography and the nature-writing genre, including environmental and ecologically focused writing. These workshops were a getaway from the Los Angeles urban setting where young writers could get inspired by the natural world.

WriteGirl volunteer Jennah Ferrer-Foronda lent her creativity and passion for photography to help spearhead this special summer workshop series and work with our teen girls to help them shift their perspectives and share their points of view with others.

The photo on the left was taken by WriteGirl mentee Indigo Mapa, age 14. As you look at the photography in the next few pages, consider how you can rethink your smartphones as a tool for art, rather than a distraction from it, and start planning a trip to nature with your pens and journals — whether it's a park near your home, a beach day or a half-day hike. Who knows what you'll be inspired to create?

Coral Lights
Aida Castelblanco
Age 15

Spotlight
Aida Castelblanco
Age 15

Aida Castelblanco, age 15

"During the Huntington photography workshops, I learned that with the right angle and lighting, you can take a picture of the most mundane thing in the world and make it new and exciting. That point of view applies to writing too. If you want to write a story about a tree or a fire hydrant or a donut, all you need to do to make your story unique and captivating is take that seemingly boring object and write about it from an angle that no one has ever tried before."

Writing Experiment

What everyday objects do you often touch or use, but take for granted? Select an object from your life — maybe it's your toothbrush or a favorite hoodie — and imagine all the ways this object might be seen as unique or captivating. What's the story that has yet to be told about your object?

Statue
Taya Kendall
Age 16

Taya Kendall, age 16

"Taking photos at The Huntington helped me visualize my writing a lot more than before. I'm a very visual person, so being able to literally see what I'm writing about helped me add more levels of detail to my pieces. I think since the photography workshops, I've been more inspired to write about things I see so that I'm able to be more descriptive and help readers see what I'm seeing."

Writing Experiment

Many poets are inspired by visual arts and images. Look at the image here. What do you see? What is the character looking at? What sound does her instrument make? How do her clothes feel or move around her? Write a poem about this image, or find another image of fine art or a sculpture that inspires you. Remember to imagine all of the senses: sight, sound, smell, touch and even taste.

The Versatility of Seasons
Courtney Hayforth
Age 17

"Originally this picture wasn't in black and white, obviously, but I started playing with the filters, and I think it just looks more appealing this way. I called it 'The Versatility of Seasons' because I wrote a poem about the contrasting characteristics of the picture. This absence of color makes it seem cold and wintry while all the leaves, plants and flowers make it seem more inviting — as if it's asking you to enter this passage with an unknown destination.

I'm a really visual person, so whenever I write, it helps me to look at a picture or a passage or story someone else wrote and get inspiration from that. This was even better because I got to actively seek out these beautiful scenes and settings and capture them myself. I think the experience of doing that made my writing more personal and emotional."

Writing Experiment

As the artist describes it, the image here features a "passage with an unknown destination." Imagine that stepping through this passageway will transform you in some way, or deliver you to a new destination. Whom do you want to become? Where do you want to go? What type of transformation would you like to experience in your life? Write about stepping through this passage and what you learn when you arrive on the other side.

Thematic Californian
Rachel Alarcio
Age 15

"One morning during winter break, I was in a poetry slump. I decided to switch gears and try my hand at writing song lyrics. I turned to my reservoir of inspiration: my photo gallery. The album's title was 'CLICK!' — photos created in the summer of 2016 during the WriteGirl workshops at The Huntington. I scrolled through old snapshots with fresh eyes, as I usually did with my poems. However, unlike with poetry, I couldn't remember why I took the photos in the first place. The more I thought and stared, the more depth I discovered beyond the beautiful facade.

Inspired by a dramatic shot of a palm tree taken at The Huntington, I set out to write a song. To my surprise, I used poetry brainstorming techniques. For instance, I sketched out bubble maps and used word association to come up with the next line in the song. When I finally did return to poetry, I noticed improvement in my internal rhyme and meter."

Writing Experiment

Word association and brainstorming can surprise us with ideas and images that come to us in an instant. Place a simple word like "tree" or "shadow" in the center of your journal page. What does the word make you think of? Write whatever comes to mind. Look at what you've written and then consider where it takes you next. Write down what the next idea makes you think of, or what it reminds you of. Avoid writing in straight lines, just continue adding thoughts, words and ideas and randomly place them all over the page. On a new page, begin a poem by gathering words, phrases and ideas from your word-association experiment.

It's Not That Scary
Indigo Mapa
Age 14

Nature Without Color
Indigo Mapa
Age 14

Indigo Mapa, age 14

"When I attended the photography workshops, it was like a dream. I knew that I had the ability to write well. My writing improved and became more personal than ever. While I quietly wrote in the gardens, I finally found a piece of myself. I finally realized what I wanted to do in life. It was like my 花樣年華 (*hwa yang yeon hwa*), or my most beautiful moment in life. It was beautiful because I found my happiness and I found myself."

Writing Experiment

Life's beautiful moments can be grand, like celebrating a graduation, or simple, like watching the sunset with a good friend. Make a list of beautiful moments from your own life, and then close your eyes and picture one of them. Who is there? What does it smell, sound and look like? How do you feel? Write a short prose poem about your beautiful moment. Try to describe how you feel without using the actual name of your feeling. Show the reader how you feel.

High Noon Shadow Down
Noelle Cope
Age 18

Noelle Cope, age 18

"I found a new perspective on my writing. Our workshop leader Jennah taught us to be fearless with our photography: take pictures from all different angles, even take blurry photos. It made me realize my writing didn't always have to be so neat and tidy. Some stories or moments need to be a little messy or blurry.

I learned in these workshops that all forms of expression are connected, that we all have our own unique talent and point of view. I learned to experiment and find new ways to tell my stories."

Writing Experiment

As the artist pointed out, writing can be messy. Think of an early memory, when you were a small child. In your journal, draw a picture of the memory. You don't have to be good at drawing. You can even make it so messy that perhaps only you can understand it. Once you're done, look closely at your memory. What part of it grabs your attention? Why? Write about your past, inspired by this "messy" memory.

9

Place

THE SILENCE OF LEE AVENUE

This poem was inspired by a photograph of Butte, Montana, taken in 1970 from a book entitled Friedlander *at the Pasadena Public Library during a WriteGirl workshop.*

Butte, Montana

Lee Avenue, desert
abandoned like a sidecar to a town
forgotten
they left the power lines,
just in case,
left the roads and light poles and fences
sidewalk, gravel, shrubs
they left the mountains,
still standing guard over Lee Avenue.
twice a year a '58 Chevy
dusty baby blue
gravel under tread,
twice a year Grandpa breaks
the silence of Lee Avenue
to reminisce.
he comes home with splinters
in his teeth, with rundown
memories, he comes home
after leaving the mountains
leaving the shrubs and gravel and sidewalks
fences, light poles, roads
leaving the power lines
on Lee Avenue.

London

And the world was upside down.
Cobblestone roads close to my face,
I could smell the history,
poverty and power,
crown jewels and stones with peasants past
spinning on the axis of Shakespeare's globe.
I was in the image of London's eye
coming up from the underground
and the world was upside down.

Cindy Liu, age 15

I had an image of a man standing in the ruins of a burned down house, and I built a story around that image.

The Fire

Yesterday, the house was full of whispers and shufflings as the mother and daughter stuffed ten years of memories into faded suitcases. Now there is just the faint crackle of embers shivering under piles of rubble as it slowly burns itself out. The house — a skeleton of charred bones — trembles in the slight breeze as footsteps crunch in the gravel. A man limping down the dilapidated sidewalk of the neighborhood walks between the smoking rubble to what remains of the house.

Itzhak stands outside, looking into the house he once knew. It has been five years since he left his family. He closes his eyes and breathes in the smoky air, trying to recall the faces of his wife and daughter that blurred with every passing year. There is something wet on his cheeks when he opens his eyes, and he stands still for a moment, blinking away the faces of his family.

Itzhak hesitates as he moves to leave, glancing back at the house. In the light of the setting sun, his silhouette is outlined in a soft fire as he shuffles and clears his throat. Quietly, the sound strangely loud in the empty air, he hums a few notes, his voice rusty and cracked.

It's a lullaby — one he heard his daughter often sing to herself as she fell asleep. The words have faded from his mind, but as he starts humming, the melody resurfaces in his mind. For a moment, there is nothing but the whispered music as it slips over his tongue.

By the time he turns to leave, his tears have dried stiff streaks into the soot that settled on his face. He doesn't look back when he walks down the cracked sidewalk, away from the smoking carcass of the house.

Yell from the
rooftops!
Be yourself.

Granada

The roofs of those towers were clothed in shingles, red like oxidized blood, delicately overlapping one another, and ambiguously wood or stone. The walls were not dressed in the portraits of noble kings and queens, but in exquisite Arabic lettering, etched and painted onto the surface in opalescent turquoise and gold, which were glistening stars in the sunlight. The once sharp edges were now worn soft and round by wandering fingertips on the grandiose arches. At the core, a vast clearing, where the concrete floors were, too, decorated with intricate carvings. In the middle, a fountain encircled by lion dog statues, steadfast guardians, follow you with their eyes. If you dared approach, you could see the sky reflected perfectly in the fountain waters, the soft cerulean rippling like fabric as gentle breezes brush through. Through the windows, the rolling hills of Spain.

This is a description of the theater and what nights are like for those of us who spend our time there.

Theater Lights

Usually the doors are shut and the red faux-velvet seats folded up, the entryway dark and the front desk closed. Slowly a group of chatty people turns on the lights, opens the curtains and tests the sound.

For hours we'll sing, dance and laugh. When the dark sweeps through the sky and the streetlights come on, we'll have to stop, turn the lights off, close up the desk, shut off the sound and lock the doors. Once again it's quiet, and no one would guess the life that can inhabit it.

On show nights we get into place and jitter with excitement. As the houselights dim, the curtains rise to reveal people who shine and sing, dance and dramatize, people who can be anyone and anything.

The light in your face, the clicking of characters' shoes — the music and sound and feeling of confidence surround you. As the chance to share with others comes to a close, you can feel the heat and excitement in the next person's hand as they grasp yours. You take the next person's and so on until you have made a train of people and you bow to the crowd that's happily clapping and cheering.

Once again the curtains must close, the lights go off and the doors lock. Outside, people won't give a second glance, not knowing they just passed a part of a cycle, the part where the light and life is gone. Still, it is what it's always been, and will bring joy, light and life again.

Ariana Cortez, age 16

I wrote this piece in Mexico while sitting on my grandma's porch.

Hermosa

Sitting on a bench,
my Converse dangling off the edge,
I sway my heels back and forth.
Sounds flow through my ear,
like warm water through my hands.
A draft of air travels through a maze.
It sprinkles my face gently like silk on skin.
Soon night falls onto the mandarin trees,
like leaves in winter, slowly then all at once.
Crickets come out of hiding,
birds willow away,
dreaming of the morning's breath.
Nature too beautiful to forget.

Sophie Anastas, age 16

I wrote this piece to whisk people away to a moment that I thought was enjoyable and exciting. It was inspired by a night out that I spent with my best-friend in a place we hadn't experienced in a long time.

City of Lights

A flood of eager bodies encompasses us
as we walk through a kaleidoscope of bright neon lights.

The sound of hopeful young artists' melodic words and guitar strums
bleed into the storefront music that we have heard far too many times before,
creating a brilliant whirlwind of sound.

It was a night spent poured over sugary sweet morsels
and long-awaited laughs.

A nostalgia that seemed to dissipate
along with everything that existed outside of the vibrant diminutive city.

Celine Merino, Age 17

I went to visit my mother's hometown in Michoacán during winter break and we went to a little island called Janitzio. There, I watched this dance for the first time.

Danza de los Viejitos

I walked alongside locals and tourists as they circled a pair of dancers. A child stood by as an older dancer slapped his feet against the pavement, the wooden bottoms of his shoes echoing loudly, his movements in sync with the violinist's upbeat tune.

The mask that concealed his face was what caught my attention the most, its bizarre expression more amusing than frightening — though the child crying next to me said otherwise. The violin suddenly shifted into something more somber, the dancer's hunched back lurching forward even more as his movements ceased.

It reflected some sort of sadness, a bit of despair and hopelessness. Then the music was upbeat again, along with the dancer. The boy, who'd stood out of his way, decided to step in, mimicking the older man's motions. His tiny shoes slapped along the concrete, creating a rhythm that was in sync with the music but differed from what the elder was trying to do.

This was my mother's culture, and I couldn't help but feel a sense of pride from the beautiful show.

Make your words strong
and loud and defiant;
never make them small.

Louana Garraud, age 16

*This piece is about the first New Year's Eve I spent
back in France since I moved to Los Angeles.*

A Night in Paris

It's only ten as I walk in
still not knowing anybody.

Unknown faces, places,
but we'll be part of history.
Smells and noises
slowly making their way to me.

Bubbles pop,
set tongues wagging,
and some boy tells me his story.

We speak our minds,
what do we care,
music will drown our honesty.

Raising our glass,
counting from ten in unity.

The clock now rests.
Put on our vests,
leaving — the night will forget me.

We live.
Youth of Paris.
The first of January.

At the WriteGirl Poetry Workshop at the Pasadena Public Library,
I browsed through the geography section, pulled out a book and
read a powerful sentence about the country Benin.

Benin

On deserted beaches
driftwood and seaweed
walk along the sand
taking over the passage
where slave ships once sailed

polluting the water
as it is now
beginning its transformation
for a free wave that beats on the lives
of the new generation

stunning indigenous architecture
of solid homes that stay bold in colors
stubborn in their own existence
as the sea and land
become fiercely unrelenting.

10
Music

A FEW SCRATCHES ON THE GROOVES

Sammy Park, age 16

Being a feminist and a multi-dimensional person allows me the freedom to be myself, regardless of norms.

Liking Pop Music Is Radical

In a society
that judges teenage girls
for everything,
being authentically "you"
is a challenge.

Music,
clothes,
even speech by girls
are policed
by a patriarchal society.

And so when I love
Fifth Harmony publicly,
or Ed Sheeran's new album,
I am well aware
of the consequences.

I am through
trying to defy
every gender
expectation
set before me.

Yes, I like pop music
and have an affinity
for pop culture.
That does not make me
any less
of a feminist.

I thought about the main way that I connect to music — for me that's when I'm either having a great or not-so-great day.

How to Feel Better with Melody

When the day is long, you come home, slip the door shut, listening for the turn and click of the doorknob. You wash yourself of conformity with the large sweater-like cloth back into what you know, what has rhythm and tempo. Mood lighting is key: soft purples and pinks with hints of warm bright light of the slow-melting sandalwood and sage. Note the vintage scratch as the needle cascades from your fingertips to the record.

Sway at first, letting the euphoric sense of calm wrap around like the warmth of a friend you've waited too long to see. The lyrics roll off your tongue, speaking for every tear, every scream. Arms, shoulders and hips swinging much like your mother's did. Let your body double over, allowing your tears to hit the ground. Eventually your body will begin to thrash, taking no precaution of the objects around you. You will know when you are done when your legs collapse, the music stops, and you are out of breath.

Olivia Trollinger, age 17

*I wrote this in a coffee shop while some upbeat jazz music was playing.
I couldn't tell you what song — I'm not a jazz aficionado.*

here's jazz

Longsleeve Rhoda permed and
porched out on a rocking chair,
the sun low and golden
under the eyes of the other mothers.
"She accumulates from time to time (at night) every night:
You'll only see it if she finds you unlucky.
And I'll tell you a secret:
What comes from milk poured warm
over equal sacrifice?"

Cindy Liu, age 15

Music I Remember

Faded photograph I take out and dust off.
My fingers twitch as they recall the
smooth coldness of the black and white keys of the piano,
and suddenly I am alive with the
woody scent of rosin dust beneath the hairs of the violin bow
as it swirls through my veins, and
the faint metallic scent of violin strings
on fingertips stained with stripes of gray.

Some days, I forget
the way my bones tremble in the sound of music.
On those days, I sit in this stranger's body
that doesn't shiver in the pulsating chords and
vibration of strings.

Today, I remember music like a resurfacing
memory I catch as it slips through
the cracks of my cupped hands.

Katherine Pyne-Jaeger, age 16

I wrote this piece recently after watching a performance of Man of La Mancha *at a local community theater. The woman playing the musical's main female role had an exceptionally striking presence I'd never noticed in an actress — a feral, tenacious and fundamentally unashamed sense of self. For those unfamiliar with the musical, during the finale, said actress leads the cast in a reprise of its most famous number (most of you will at least have heard of "The Impossible Dream," I don't doubt). While I watched, for a moment before the houselights went down, her face looked as if something holy had struck it: her eyes were like those of Saint Teresa in Bernini's* Ecstasy. *I understood with complete certainty that I needed to attempt to preserve that in a poem. The title refers to Saint Cecilia, Roman martyr beheaded in Sicily and patroness of musicians.*

Cecilia

A woman with the body
of a lion sang. Something
began to stream forth from
the forge door of her eyes.
It was her soul.
It lifted briefly,
Sublimely,
out of the dark.

A song is what-
ever you want it
to be — you just
have to give it
your soul.

Talia Kazandjian, age 16

Truthfully, a One Direction song inspired this piece. I was reminiscing about when I was a crazy fan at the age of 12 and how much I have grown since then. This just goes to show that no matter how hard I try to escape my awkward preteen years, they always come back to haunt me.

Shuffle

Life tries to knock you down sometimes, and if not sometimes, all the time. There are days when you can't handle the simple stress of school or work. There are other days when things that you wanted so badly to work out are suddenly not going the way you planned. There are even days when all you want to do is just break down and cry because you simply cannot take another second before something else goes wrong. On these days, sometimes music is a breath of fresh air, the light at the end of the tunnel, whether uplifting or depressing.

The familiar chords and the soft sound of the piano suddenly take you away from all your problems, to your happy place. The catchy pop tune that your favorite boy band sang takes you to when you were 12, giggling with your friends in your bedroom over a silly crush you had. This overplayed song that you loved so much gives you this overwhelming feeling of nostalgia, making you wish you were that young once again. Or the heavy sound of the drums and guitar, along with the scratchy voice of the singer from your good-for-nothing worthless college boyfriend's favorite band, takes you back to a place where you felt worthless yourself, a place you do not want to go back to.

Feelings follow, good and bad, tied to the songs that you listen to on a daily basis and reminders that what you're going through is temporary. It's a reminder that life has been better and has also been worse. It is a reminder everything happens for a reason, and that is simply the way of life. Every happy song you've listened to will come again on shuffle, and unfortunately the sad songs will too.

Sometimes I like to go to punk shows to yell and forget about sad things.

The Pit

You couldn't be self-conscious in the pit; it wouldn't let you. All you could do was throw yourself into the sound of the music, hard drums pulsating with lines that weren't melodic but that you forced yourself to chant along because you couldn't help yourself.

It wasn't always like this. Sometimes you would encounter the guy who pushes just to shove and likes to pull girls' ponytails. Other times the aural chaos helped in self-reflection — the only time you could think independently was when everyone else was drowning themselves out.

So you strum strum strum, E F G, E F G, harmonies made from dissonance made from the intention behind anarchy. You couldn't be self-conscious in the pit; it wouldn't let you.

Diana Balbuena, age 16

This poem was written after thinking about the definition of music.

Beats and Tempo

The elegance of the violin,
the harmony of the piano,
the strum of the guitar.
The sound of music
beats and tempo.

I might not always listen to all the world's music —
but I hear it in the streets echoing in earphones;
I see it painted on murals saying, "I will always love you."

It lies deep within all of us,
heard around the world:
jazz, pop, rock, R&B, cumbia, salsa, rap and merengue.
Different tones and connotations
like the colors of a rainbow,
apart yet highlighting individuality, each color contrasting.
Music.

Writing about personal experiences is nothing to be afraid of.

Samantha Krug, age 13

This scene was inspired by Phantom of the Opera.

The Room on the Left

Amethyst hears the melodies and harmonies of the piano coming from the room on the left. She knows she's not allowed in, but she's curious: why is it so dangerous? Finally, she opens the door and steps tentatively inside.

A figure hunches over the piano, fingers gliding over the keys. The melody is soft and tender, and Amethyst remembers how she used to pick daisies, alone, at school. The melody slowly grows in tempo, the bass line crescendoing louder and fiercer until Amethyst gasps. The figure immediately stops and tenses, finally sensing her presence. She steps out of the darkness and then notices who the figure is: her mother.

It couldn't be possible, Amethyst thinks, tears forming in her eyes.

"Amethyst? You really shouldn't be here. It's too early," her mother says, starting to cry.

Amethyst immediately rushes to her mother's side, afraid.

"This room is a portal to the Fields of Elysium. You entered the Underworld when you stepped inside."

This piece started as a quickly written sestina for school but turned into a poem about music and the need for freedom of speech.

My Music

I am brittle in a place without sound,
only echoes of my voice
ricocheting off walls without passion.
I am nil with the absence,
for my soul and music are intertwined
in a ballad of mesmerized gazes —
a murmur, a light vibrato, a thumping heart.

There can be no sort of warmth from accidental grazes
in this place, seemingly intertwined
a black hole, a lack of enlightenment,
swallows passion, devouring stomping feet
melody of people, cries muffled by omnipotent
silence.

Ava Chamberlin, age 14

I love to shop for old records and always wonder what they sound like, where they came from and the stories they could tell.

Discovering

Dust danced before my eyes as I stared down at rows upon rows of twelve-inch cardboard sleeves. I flipped through as many as I could. They were all black vinyl on the inside but seemed so different on the outside. Some were new and unopened, and some were tattered and well loved. All of them told a different story.

Had they been lost and forgotten in some basement, waiting for someone to pluck them out from the dark? Or had they been a cherished collection that just wasn't relevant anymore? I wondered when they had been played: at a cheerful wedding, after a breakup, or maybe during a first date?

Each one had a story behind it, and I wished I could find some way to know each and every one, but I was on a budget after all, so I'd have to get to know only two. I decided to find the most tattered and worn sleeves with graphics fading from being eagerly handled so many times. There would be a few scratches on the grooves, but I didn't mind. If they were ripped and taped back together, I knew that they had to be good, that they probably contained someone's favorite songs. Listening to someone's cherished songs would allow me to know not only the album but the person who owned it as well.

As I picked my final two, I wondered, would these records end up at another place just like this one, and would someone come pick them out and uncover a piece of me as well?

Don't be afraid to use old memories and ideas in new writing works. (Reduce, reuse, and recycle) :)

11
Love

CAN'T BRING MY HEART TO SKIP YOU

Every seven years, all cells in the human body are slowly replaced with new ones. Although this is an incredibly interesting scientific fact, it's also heartbreaking at the same time.

Seven Years

"Did you know, after seven years, every cell in the human body is replaced?"

It was the first thing you ever said to me. I don't know if it was meant to be an interesting fact or some sort of jolting hook for the life you were living, but I was intrigued.

I think that was how our friendship worked. You would say something abrupt, and I would be fascinated.

"That can't be true," I would say, my head leaning against my palm, my eyes wide with curiosity.

And then you would rattle on about how, yes, of course that was true and, yes, you had found it on the internet, but when was the internet ever wrong? And light bulbs would go off over your head and you'd wave your arms around as you spoke, and I had never seen anything as breathtakingly magnificent in my entire life.

And it went on for seven years.

I learned about everything from black toothpaste (and the fact that it cleaned better than regular toothpaste), to the gold paint on the edges of books, to the effects of singing as soon as you woke up in the morning, to the legitimate size that wings would have to be if human beings were meant to fly.

And then you were gone.

And I was left saying, "That can't be true," to a silence that was indescribable. To people who didn't have the secrets of the universe tucked away into an impossible number of pockets in their brains. People whose eyes didn't light up when they figured out the fastest way to tie their own shoes.

Now almost seven years have passed. And it breaks my heart to know that I will soon have a body that you will have never touched.

The thing about revision is that nobody likes it but everybody needs it.

Mayra Blas, age 18

I wrote this about relationships.

Same Old, Same Old

You and me, a song on repeat
engraved into my brain
I already know the words you're going to say

The time of day doesn't matter
You sing
I still sing along
(as if it weren't an overplayed song)

I can't bring my heart to skip you
Your beat keeps it dancing
your sweet melody

I hear the beginning of your song
and every time

I can't help but hope
you'll only ever sing it
to me

Mozart Dee, age 17

I was inspired by the colors gold and red and how they are everywhere.

Burnt Sugar and Black Coffee

Your eyes crash into my eyes,
like the ocean they break.
You stand so close
I can see the flecks of gold
that outline your irises,
putting your soul on display
like a Degas painting at the Louvre.

You smell like burnt sugar and black coffee.
I don't like black coffee.
I don't like you.
You shift your gaze away.
I see the reflection of the sun
for a moment
in your eyes.
They flash crimson,
and I remember.

The Girl Who Loved Herself

"It wasn't love," she tells her friends.
"There was heat but no spark
when we locked eyes."

She liked to lie to herself,
repeating "I love you" with uncertainty.

I love you?
I love you.
I love you …

No. She doesn't love him.
She loves the idea of loving and being loved,
but she doesn't love him.

"I'm sorry, please forgive me!"
Yet how could he when he knew
the woman he loved just couldn't love him back?

Contrary to popular belief, she can love.
She does love. She is loving.

She loves herself and her life,
and nobody can blame her for that.

Saenah Boch, age 17

I wrote this for my childhood friend Yume, whose name means "Dream" in Japanese.

Dream

They parked the car at the top of the hill and let the engine idle, watching the clouds keel over to a Blondie cassette, but their minds somewhere else, untouchable, daydreaming *impending dooms* and *what ifs*, bare feet playing footsie with the grass, a refuge for unwanted Blue Moons and crushed Camel stubs. Her big toe locked lips with his ankle; his elbow poked her hair as the crook of his armpit swallowed her head. She turned his palm over in her own and stared at his busted calluses and remembered all of a sudden what it felt like to be in love.

Kayla Veloz, age 14

I wanted to explore the topic of love, cliché and all, from multiple points of view.

Like Summer

It's ice cream day.
A melody plays through the walls —
vanilla, chocolate, and have you tried bubblegum?

The raging heat melts every aspect of the day —
a bee's buzz and a bird's chirp.
Ice cream drips down your hand.

You love it and hate it all the same.
You are a reminder of that,
not in my plans, but in my mind.

Like a pounding musical beat,
my favorite song, yet overplayed,
you are like summer.

Hanna Lucia Maaloul, age 13

This song is about a boy that I liked a little while back.

Forwards and Back

Your eyes
are the ocean.
They pull me forward
and back.
Your eyes
get me
lost.
Your
eyes
find
me.

At a WriteGirl workshop, I wrote about a moment I wish I could have captured on film: before my girlfriend and I were dating, and we were in the musical together.

Indigo

Midnight silhouettes separated by the importance of plot.
I never appreciated how soft your hands were
until they let go of mine.
Actors onstage shouting words they never wanted to have said.
Soaring crescendos of diametric opposition could not keep
their smoldering grip on stolen glances in the darkness
behind closed curtains. The line is blurred.
Where their world stops and our world ends
no longer holds the power once given to it.
A heart seeps through, battered and bloody, shedding crimson spatters
into the glassy blackness they don't want you to see.
Between longing and repulsion there is a beat.
A thunder, cacophonous and loud, the revolting plea
of wanting to be seen. Of desire. Of disgust.
Of please look at my ugly parts but please see me.
Wanting to stay away but not wanting to let go.
Pay no attention to what goes on behind the curtain.
The swan song of blooming affection.
Broad sweeping fire and pitched passions unseen by the light of day.
You let go; we share a glance and go to our places.

Poems are best started
when you have a strong
emotion forcing its way
through you.

When you fall in love, you fall hard, so any barrier between you and that person will seem possible to overcome.

Violet Eyes

Mysterious you may be, but
I'm determined to unveil
the mystery that is you.

Your beauty makes
light shine upon you.

The magic you possess
can't compare to
the magic of your charm.

In your violet eyes
that shine in the night,
I see shards of glass.
The roses call out to you.

Brandy Mendoza, age 17

This poem started off as an English project but ended up being so much more.

Space Odyssey

Gravity is strange.
We don't know how it works.
It attracts, just like love.

If you stand still, you can't see
gravity's effects in motion.
You have to jump, which requires force.

Love is massive. Love takes force
to bring it to great heights.
Love causes colors to fade into your mind.

But if you meet someone special,
love grows endless like the vast eternity of space.

Ayanna Jackson, age 17

Recently I have felt very numb to a lot of things.

Numb

I went looking for something
wherever I could find it.
When you came into my life
I was almost blinded.
But now I can't feel
anything remotely real.
I truly need to be reminded.

Jayda Crawford, age 15

The inspiration for this poem is heartbreak.

Nothing but Thorns

He was standing in the rain
dressed like a matador
She thought it was a dream
She picked up a rose

Every petal can be broken
All the beauty can be
gone
All that was left was
nothing but thorns

We can all be standing
in front of the same
thing but see it
differently.

Jay Shillingford, age 18

I wrote this in a WriteGirl workshop and edited it many times over with my mentor at the time. I wrote it because I was trying to dig deep and find out how I could paint a picture with words, to have the reader see what I felt. I wrote it for my girlfriend and for myself.

Last I Saw You

You were walking away. It was warm and sunny, but cold air came like whiplash to my face and heart. I felt time slowing and my eyes burning and stinging. The grass felt hollow between my fingertips and the air smelled salty. I kept thinking, how long until I see you again, as you started to slip from my gaze.

The last hug from you was a comforting cup of tea that filled me up with overwhelming warmth. I knew that too soon you and I needed to go separate ways, and I fought the tears that threatened to spill. One more thought of this bittersweet memory and I won't be able to watch you leave without me. The truth is, as I saw your back turning and you walking quickly, we both knew that if you didn't leave fast enough you'd be stuck with me forever.

Isabel Alejandra Aguirre, age 17

I wanted to write about a couple I saw when I was with my father fishing at Venice Beach. The couple was dancing along the boardwalk, and when she saw me sitting there while my dad fished she approached. Without saying a word she offered me the rose I presume her partner gave her. I was about ten years old.

The Rose

I gazed at the couple down the boardwalk.
They were there,
dancing and twirling together.
All I could do was stare.

They held one another softly,
as if this were the last time they would see each other.

He was like a dream.
And she was the one.
A couple made from above.

Slowly they both leaned in …
her cheeks a soft rose and his eyes which held pure love.

Two inches close,
the kiss a mixture of fireworks
and then warmth blossoming within her.
Then she glanced at me and smiled warmly.

I remember this day and don't want it to fade,
the day a woman in love gave me a rose.
This memory of love,
which keeps me hopeful to this day.

This song isn't about anyone specifically;
it just kind of came to me.

Forget Me Not

Verse
I like the way you look in my eyes
You are my sun, and you always rise
You keep me happy and filled with hope
You are the one who keeps me afloat

Chorus
And I like your eyes, like water drops
I like your words and pretty thoughts
Love me now, forget me not
Love me now, forget me not

Verse
I like the flowers in your hair
I like the way you're standing there
I like your smile in the dark
Your soft voice singing like a lark

Chorus
And I like your eyes, like water drops
I like your words and pretty thoughts
Love me now, forget me not
Love me now, forget me not

Walking around the lily ponds in the gardens at The Huntington inspired this poem.

Love Triangle

My heart is broken in two,
half is with me and half is with you.
I hope your heart is broken in two,
and that half is with me and half is with you.

But
her heart is broken in two,
half is with her and half is with you.
And your heart is broken in two,
half is with her and half is with you.

Lock your phone away
when you write.

Love

Love strikes away the heartache.
Love strikes away the fear of loneliness.
Yet we can't get enough of love —
we lust for it every second of our being.
Love is a shapeshifter —
one second, it's an open window,
then another second,
it's an unreachable object.

12

Resist

SUIT UP, SPEAK UP, RISE UP

Gillian Chamberlin, age 13

This song was inspired by the election and men not respecting women.

Please Don't Talk to Me Like That

Verse
Please don't talk to me like *that*
acting like your heart's so big.
I've been here before,
I've been down that road,
so please don't talk to me like *that*.

Chorus
You try to drag me in,
into your muddy world,
but I keep turning you down saying,
please don't talk to me like *that*.

Verse
Your T-shirt's covered in crocodile tears.
Your gray eyes as big as the moon,
you beg for forgiveness but I only reply,
please don't talk to me like *that*.

I wrote this during my first WriteGirl workshop responding to a prompt that said "statistics."

5'3"

I am 5'3"
towering over Filipino boys like the *Burj Khalifa*,
making me an undesirable selection to preserve their pride.

I am 5'3"
too big, too bulky.
My family says, "When I was your age, I was petite!
Light enough so that men could swallow me whole.
So I can be safe in the pits of their inflated bellies
that matched their inflated pride.
I was small enough to be wanted,
to be an appetizer for their patriarchal hunger."

"While you," they mock, "you are too big to fit into their mouths.
You rip through their arrogant intestines.
You are not weak enough. You must be weak enough."

But I am 5'3" and I know two things:
My body is too big for my dwarfed confidence.
The tallest building in the world is not the *Burj Khalifa*, 2,722'.

It is me.
5'3" and unable to be swallowed whole.

Taylor Blackwell, age 18

I went to the Women's March and saw the following on a girl's poster: "We are the granddaughters of the witches you couldn't burn at the stake."

Witches Wanted

Coincidence, chaos, clockwork cycles
Moon's guidance magnetizes us
Visions of infinity, epiphanies informing our insanities
Alchemists, astrophysicists, arrogance checked at archways
Don't fear unknown spheres, planes of existence
Ingenious pursuits persevere persistence
Hex, curse, magic love on Earth

We Rise

The bubbles rise,
a single stream.
Smaller and smaller,
its origin
farther and farther.

A failed attempt.
Another cry.
Another heartbeat.
We're falling,
hand in hand.

Stronger than the pain,
we fight together.
We fall as one,
the light returns,
we rise.

You can do anything
you want with the
words you put on a
page. They're yours.

Jyla Yu, age 15

I wrote this poem to reflect on what's going on in the United States of America today.

Orchestra

We've been singing for years now.
Everyone has known their part
through trial and error,
through failure and triumph.

Now this new conductor wants to come around
and tell us we're wrong,
that we're off-key, that we're off-tone.
He's changing the orchestra,
putting us here and them there.

Will we ever get our rhythm back?
Does he know we've been singing the same song?
Conductor after conductor,
justice and liberty for all.

Illusions

Verse 1
Peaceful thoughts make peaceful dreams
Let the nightmares slip away
Their loss is your own gain
No more resets, not today

Chorus
Fears are works of your own mind
You can escape them and try to find
New hopes and dreams to prevent intrusion
We all know fears are just illusions

Verse 2
Peaceful thoughts will ease the pain
Don't stress anymore, my dear
Let peace and love fill your soul
Let all these worries disappear

Chorus
Fears are works of your own mind
You can escape them and try to find
New hopes and dreams to prevent intrusion
We all know fears are just illusions

Think you are done?
Read it out loud!

Prickly

These plants remind me of you because you are prickly. You were born in the desert, so you grew thick skin and a million defense mechanisms. These plants remind me of you because they have to grow tall to be safe enough to flower. They have to be strong to be vulnerable. These plants remind me of you because you can see beauty in things that no one else would think to see at first glance. These plants remind me of you because you told me that to live is your biggest rebellion against those who want you dead. Because they are stubbornly clinging to water in the driest places this world has to offer.

These plants remind me of you because they're beautiful in the most idiotic way.

Rise Up

They'll try to stop your flight,
try to pull you down.

But you can't hear them,
won't feel them.
Poisons of the past
just roll off your body.

And you see it all:
the joy, the love, the hope.
And you rise
to your best self.

You rise and rise
up, above anything.
You have arrived,
your soul warm and bright.

Capture the reader with
the action and details.

Writer's Block

Her metallic ring, size six, sat stagnant at the edge of the table
and waves of her hair were thrown hastily from her eyes.
Pen in hand and determination in her face,
she glared at the paper in front of her.
One single piece of crisp, white paper: her enemy.
For an hour, she had crumpled the papers one by one,
all destined to the bin beside her.
Her brain was filled with a myriad of abstract thoughts and
images of
incomprehensible puzzles,
untranslatable to words on paper.
The smell of blue ink was no stranger to her,
her hands punctured by the pen.
She took a sharp breath, once again defeated.
Looking around the room, she saw her battlefield,
and at once, she began to write anew.

If I Have a Daughter

If I have a daughter, I will tell her that the dark-skinned girls with tight curls like us are no less than the rest; we are brown beauty queens.

That our gay and trans sisters are as worthy as we, as human as she, as women as me.

That true Christians fear God not those with a hijab.

If I have a daughter, I will tell her that we are people.

We are people living for the American Dream, and ICE agents have badges where their hearts should be. We are humans, living in this beautiful place and "alien" is only relevant when referring to space.

If I have a daughter, I will tell her that we — bronze, brown, beige, all beautiful — hold a voice, a presence, a choice, a weapon. I will not teach her to kneel down, stand down, chin down, sit down. I will teach her to suit up, speak up, stand up and rise up.

If I have a daughter, I will tell her that her skirt is no sexual invitation. Gender can't dictate her goals or aspirations. Her body is hers, not his definition. The sky is the minimum, and never the limit.

I will say, pledge allegiance to the United States flag and be loyal to the majority of which we stand: one nation, divided, with liberty and justice for few privileged to it.

If I have a daughter, I will say don't make America great again, make America great for once. Reject walls that segregate nations, and build bridges that unify people. Because no human can be born unequal.

If I have a daughter, if I have a son, if I have a child who is both or none, I will raise them to know there is no us or them, them and us.

There is us and us and us and us.

13

Nature / Science

LULLABY OF AN AWAKENED STORM

Bioluminescence

Plankton
stealthy sea drifters
that often go unnoticed
unseen, undetected,

invisible
to the naked eye.

But when their calm world
is disrupted
by late-night divers
invading their lightless world,

they flare up
outshine every organism around them
provide light to guide all those
who tread past them.

Like great friends
who go unseen
dipping in and out
of people's lives
but rise to the occasion
to provide light.

Bioluminescent
in moments of darkness.

I was sitting outside of my school and began to notice all of the sounds around me. I especially noticed the construction noises.

The World

Put down the device and notice the world.
Notice the noises, the sounds.
Notice everything.

Notice all of them: melodies, undertones,
percussive-like thuds.
Notice the hums, barely audible
in the midst of other noises.

Notice the silence fills the space around you.
The petals of flowers, colorful vibrancy,
cracks in the pavement…

Notice how all the elements form a perfectly
imperfect little picture, a bubble
in a moment in time.

Put down the device and notice the world.

Katie Osaki, age 16

This piece was inspired by my love and hate for living in a beach city.

I Never Liked the Ocean

I never liked the ocean, not really. As a child I would sit with my chubby legs extended toward the reaching water, counting the number of times it tried to touch my feet. Back and forth, the gentle rush of melodic waves mesmerized my growing mind.

I remember the excitement I felt, the burst of jubilation, when my mom said, "I think we should go to the beach today." Just the thought of the sand rolling between my toes, and the soft, salty breeze hitting my face, made me rise from the dead.

But that rush of emotion, that shot of adrenaline that made my heart beat faster, never really brought me joy. Every time I went to the beach, I knew that I would have to go home afterward, the gravitational force pulling me back to a place I never knew.

Home was a barren world, with resentful walls that bound me to four rooms. Home was not the ocean. Home was sitting on a beach, chubby legs extended toward the reaching water that would never touch my feet, no matter how many times it tried. I never liked the ocean, not really.

When I'm faced with a blank page, I force myself to type. Even if it is nonsense, I will eventually find the words I'm searching for.

Julia Sorchini, age 16

I wrote this piece during a section of the WriteGirl Poetry Workshop where we focused on music and plants in the gardening section at the Pasadena Public Library.

Echeveria Rundelli

My eyes are deceiving
yet your whistle tone tugs me
into your captivating trance
of bassoon-like aura.

With every blow and toot,
the transverse orchestra summons
the sun's radiation.

Warmth tinges the edges of rosettes
as whimsical winds tint erect stems
sprouting from the driest soil.

This is a world you are able to escape to and forget everything.

My Own World

Here I am,
dancing to the beat of my own drum,
not wondering whose eyes are watching,
whose lips are moving.
I am in my own world where the flowers are always in bloom,
the air always crisp, the wind at a murmur,
fruit so sweet the juice, as I bite into it
runs down my arms, paints them a haunting red,
sunsets so beautiful it could make the devil cry.
I look up to darkness only to see moondust
thrown about like a splattered painting.
What brilliance it took to create that,
a masterpiece in the sky, for my eyes
and for those who choose to see it.

If you have a question, so will your reader.

Olivia Bloome, age 16

This piece is about the scariest day of my life,
when I took my sailing test at summer camp.

The Storm

It started off like every other summer day at camp. I had been studying for weeks for my advanced sailing test by capsizing my boat and getting yelled at by my instructors for hours on the water.

This day, the sun disappeared suddenly and I felt goose bumps. I was going fast, my little sailboat flying across the ocean with the instructors' motorboat far behind. My sails flapped in the wind, and my skin shivered from falling raindrops.

I knew the boat was going over. It was inevitable, and yet I was still terrified. The moment stopped in time. Seconds felt like minutes. My body slammed against the water as I felt the ocean cover every part of me like a silky, cold blanket. I felt light and also heavy. I saw the dark skies above me as the cold water surrounded me. I thought for sure I was going to sit in the frigid water for an eternity.

I snapped back and surfaced, gasping for air like a fish out of water. I moved my arms around and tried desperately to come up with a plan. I swam against the rough waters to the opposite side of my boat and pulled my freezing body back in. I knew I had to get back to camp, back to the docks, to safety. All I could do was make my boat go as fast as it could and hope for the best.

I told myself I would be fine as I crept toward the dock. My little boat pushed closer and closer to the safety of land. I was scared but my adrenaline was running high. The dock was so close I could almost touch its rough wood. I pictured my shaking body on the perfect and predictable surface of land, safety, and it finally came.

Angelica Cordova, age 17

I wrote this poem when the day had reached its end. The day had been sunny, but the warmth dissipated into cold when it began to drizzle. I thought of how the skies were brimming with rain outside. I began to admire the simple strength of the trees, how they could withstand the rain and would not shrink away from the wetness.

Tree Song

we are trees in a forest struck by lightning
replacing our song with a piercing scream
snapping our branches
roaring winds whisking away our leaves
the bark of our skin splintering and cracking
leaving us naked, bare
a skeletal remain of life
but when the rain kisses our roots
seeps into our soil like a warm blanket
and welcomes us, washes over us
we continue to grow and sing our song

This poem represents change in my life.

Rebirth

Oh so it begins.
The twisted branches
swallow them whole.
Not a trace
of the once mournful and solemn figures
that stood over the trees
and the supreme being
that existed only in the darkness.
The sweet scent of jasmine
wafts its way
through the tightly knit cages
and a new flower is born.

Juliana Pincus, age 13

One day at the beach, I took a selfie, and it reminded me of a sunflower.

Daughter Universe

I took a selfie at the beach because I was feeling at peace. I was feeling a sense of being replenished, like the sunflower does to others.

If I reach a crossroad, the present universe rises to two daughter universes. If I go to my right or if I go to my left, in each universe, I witness one or the other outcome. We are sisters in the universe, living on planet Earth yet sharing the same space, time, matter and energy. We are different but equal.

I love to heal through my arts, the way the sunflower heals by nourishing our bodies. I love hearing music in my head while making sand angels on the beach, like the sunflower that creates music through color and the sounds of singing birds that land on it, or bees when it's time to eat. Then at night when we return to sleep, we close our eyes without a peek until the next day comes, and we are awakened by sweet melodies of the day: birds chirping, my mommy calling me down for school.

I wonder how my twin is doing in the other universe. I am the Gemini twins of the universe, the daughters of Mother Earth, the daughter universes.

The sunflower is energy connecting to me to let me know we are both free — free to play, to laugh, to sing, to feel, to touch, to smell, to live, to die, to love, to express, to let go, to hang onto a vision of the creator. I fly high with sunflowers all around me.

Uma Durairaj, age 15

I wrote this poem when I came home after a WriteGirl workshop one afternoon. I was inspired by the nature in my backyard, juxtaposed with the concrete of the downtown buildings.

Earth

I hear Your dying song.
You are slowly breaking apart, shattered notes,
no way to put You back together again.

not many people understand the eerie notes You wail
about Your future. maybe they just don't care
because they won't be here to hear them.

remember the spotless skies and crisp air,
the seas of diamonds and rich earth, the lush forests.
a beautiful complex melody.

but now, electronic trance blasts in the air.
stumps where the trees once thrived,
tainted atmosphere, endangered animals —

everything a silent symphony
balancing on a tightrope,
over the abyss of extinction.

Your dirge reminds us to consider
the tragedy of Your loss;
there aren't many fighting for You,
but You must continue existing.

Aida Castelblanco, age 15

I wrote this piece at the WriteGirl Poetry Workshop with my mentor for that day. We were talking about seasons, and I just wanted to write something that expressed the happiness and simplicity of summer.

tasting the sun

lemon-crisp air and the sound of buzz,
my eyes squint through the sun-spirited summer sunrise
dripping through my overhead canopy of rippling fronds.
with great expectations in my hands,
and the black and white pattern of sunlight
and shadow across my shoulders,
summertime rests on the tip of my tongue —
like watermelons and ice and honey.

I was inspired to write this poem while listening to a piano piece called "The Girl with the Flaxen Hair." The music reminded me of a quiet day at the beach, sitting on the sand and listening to the waves.

The Ocean

It is mostly quiet on the empty beach. The waves lap gently and, of course, the sand is silent. But if you listen, past the whisper of the water, you can hear a seagull cry out, perhaps to a lost lover or just to hear the echo of his own voice.

The sound of a small crab's claws, shifting the sand by your toes, above the blue-green beauty of the water. A single sailboat breaks the calm surface and maybe you can hear the boat's lone passenger whistling a tune that is carried to your ears by the wind and on the feathers of that lonely seagull above.

The wind makes a tune of its own for you to enjoy, plays gently with your hair. The crab trips suddenly and rolls onto its back. You place two fingers underneath and gently roll it over. For a split second, you can feel its little heartbeat, its life on your hand.

The sun is slipping lower and you know that soon you must go back to cars and smoke and life. But you don't go just yet. Instead, you sit a little longer and listen to the soft song of the not-so-empty beach.

Bibiana Mashamba, age 17

Bibiana joined WriteGirl after moving to the United States from Tanzania. We asked her to share her poem in both English and Swahili.

Maua Valiyo Badirika Kuwa Ndege

Wakati was Masika maua hung'aa bustani mwangu,
Ninajisikia nimebarikiwa kuwa na maua kama haya
Ninajisikia upweke nikiwa peke yangu,
Ninakuwa Shwari nikiiona bustani na maua yake mazuri
Ninajisikia Kama niko mbinguni nina sheherekea siku ya Krismasi,
Nikiwa kwenye bustani yangu na maua mazuri yakipunga kama
Malaika, iba, kula, keki ndogo, chokoleti na vanilla ici crimu.

Ninaonja utamu wa maua katika mdomo wangu!
Naupepo ukipuliza nywele zangu upende mmoja hadi
mwingine kama maua katika bustani yangu yakiimba
Pamoja na mimi.

Mchana nilijisikia upweke kwa sababu nilikuwa peke yangu.
Nikaenda bustani ili maua yangu yaniliwaze.
Nilipoyakaribia, La hapana! maua yangu yalikuwa hayapo.
Lo mungu wangu! "angaria pale," nikajiongerea mwenyewe.
Ninaona ndege wengi wanapaa kwenye bustani yangu.
Lo hapana! Nimaua yangu, yamebadilika kuwa ndege.
Nilipomaliza kusema vile, maua yangu yakatokezea na kuanza kuimba,
"Tulikuwa maua yaliyobadirika kuwa ndege."

The Flowers Which Turned to Birds

At spring season flowers shine in my garden.
I feel blessed to have such flowers.
I feel lonely when I am alone.
I remain calm when I see my garden with its beautiful flowers.
I feel like I am in heaven celebrating Christmas
when I am in my garden and the beautiful flowers are waving like angels,
singing, eating cupcakes, chocolate or vanilla ice cream.

I taste the sweetness of the flowers in my mouth!
And the wind blowing into my hair from side to side
like the flowers in my garden singing together with me.

At noon I felt lonely because I was alone.
I went to my garden so that my flowers could give me company.
When I approached — oh NO! My flowers were gone.
Oh my God! "Look at that," I mumbled to myself.
I see many birds flying around my garden.
Oh no! It's my flowers. They had turned into birds.
After I said that, the flowers appeared and started singing,
"We were flowers which turned into birds."

Annie Bleveans, age 13

A twisted cactus inspired this song.

Twisted

Gnarled by the force
that changes her course,
she's twisted,
twisted by the wind.

She doesn't know where to swim.
She doesn't drown.
She's just standing her ground,
standing her ground.

I was flipping through a book of symbols with my mentor and came across "crows" and was captivated by their symbolism.

Crows

Crows, ministers of an elemental hush,
scrape inky bodies across a graveyard
of plum sky. The crows of crows unearth
the sacred in the savage; the artistry of skeletons
piled like white jewels; the lullaby
of an awakened storm breathes life
and noise into the same forest it will choke;
the way snake spines in deserts tuck
into the helixes of far-flung shells.

Crows, masters of unseen testimony,
dance in the palpitations of dreams we wish
we could remember, nightmares we wish
we could forget. I am terrified of crows.
Nothing about them is mistaken: not the improvisation
of saddened nature, not how they sculpt their bodies on a music
sheet of cloud, black beaks and claws translating a dirge
I am too wise, or too fearful, to sing.

Home

My wispy hair rose with the wind,
creating abstract lines while whipping around the air.
The ground beneath me, amalgamated with color, crunched beneath my fee
the footstep of one, isolated, alone.
My hand by my side, brushing the tail of my shirt as I walked,
occasionally reigned back my flapping hair.
In a year, I'll taste fall again,
but not the same as I do today.
In a year, my footsteps will not create the syncopated rhythm as they do n
But when the leaves turn mossy brown again
and the streets begin to bustle,
I'll be back,
for a short, sweet forever.

Things may not and will not turn out the way you expected, but don't be afraid of that fact.

14

Los Angeles

THE CRUCIFIX AND THE HOLLYWOOD SIGN

Ana-Mariana Sotomayor Palomino, age 16

The poem was inspired by the music and lifestyle of my community.

Inner-City Gold

Vehicular amphitheaters
you can find in the hood
one-pack of hip-hop ballads.
Every day's a concert
tuning into inner-city gold
counterfeit sheet music.
Policemen juggle harmonicas and handcuffs
waiting for somebody
to play the wrong piano key.
Discover the residue of boom boxes
cellular symphonies now in their place
observe the performance of
slouched strutting in non-gentrified L.A.
when you exhibit
those new Dickies work pants
that cost three hours
on minimum wage.

Los Angeles is stereotyped as a sunny paradise to many outsiders.

A Los Angeles Winter

The world laughs
as we moan about
darkened skies pouring drizzle
shivering in snow-free winter.

High on smog-capped mountains
snow falls from plastic boxes above.
Seasonal skiers trip
on brown dirt peeking through
so-called SoCal snow.
Children shovel handfuls of
gray sleet into their open mouths.

Hot chocolate,
of lukewarm water
and chocolate-flavored sucrose,
is too hot for sixty Fahrenheit.
Eggnog sours
à la plage
and soaks a nearby sandman.

With each sparkling rose float
and jazz-emitting trumpet,
we mourn for last year's sorrows
under the patronizing sun.

Ode to the Thomas Guide

A 1998 edition of the Thomas Guide sits under the passenger seat,
with a coffee stain baked into the pages.
It sits, forgotten, like an old favorite toy:
a doll made of rags of dirty streets
and stuffed with scraps of old neighborhoods.
My parents get upset that I don't know how to read a map,
that I rely on the robotic voice of my GPS
instead of giving the colorful webs a voice of my own.
Last week my parents found the old thing
and looked at it like a photo album,
remembering what it felt like to trace the veins of the city
with unwrinkled fingertips;
murmuring to themselves a lullaby
of left turns and freeway exits.

Kyla Walker, age 16

The beautiful city I live in inspired this piece. Walking and exploring here has shown me more of the world than I could ever imagine.

The City Wakes

She was running away
from the sun setting and the chasing waves
to find her escape in the rain.

Where clouds covered her tracks
and the wind silenced her screams
and raindrops hid away every fallen tear.

When she lost her breath, she heard the sound
of lights bleeding and a city waking,
the beat of her heart and the melody of flying traffic,
the buzz of conversation and the lyrics
in all the books she'd ever read,
and when the song ended, she felt it.

The vintage lights of a lonely street,
the dizzy eye of a Ferris wheel
and the colliding hills of our sea.

And she knew she was finally home.

I was inspired by my school and my friends.

West to East

The sun is setting on my Western tastes
like a last bite of kimchi pancakes
midnight-food-truck tacos
animal fries washed down with pink lemonade.
Feels like sore legs approaching my apartment building
last sips of Yum Yum's coffee, rushed.
Eyes jumping open to the electronic voice
"Now approaching ..." wherever.
K-Town for mochas and BBQ,
Santa Monica for shopping and ocean air.

The sun is setting on the three corners of my youth:
Melrose and Burroughs and Venice.
These are the final 30 seconds
of the hip-hop serenade
dancing in the palm trees.
One final night, finishing a robot for competition
researching a heated debate
typing out analysis on poetry
or crying onto the final pages of a Murakami novel.
I pack my bags for the next adventure
take one last look
sigh and turn my back
on a city that I claim as a town.
I become a silhouette.

Poetry is
about finding
your truth.

Catherine Shonack, age 16

I wrote this for my mom, who immigrated to the United States from Peru. She left her family and home behind for a chance at a better life. Leaving your home is not easy, and to do so knowing that you might never come back is brave.

City of Stars

She looked out at the city that was known for its famous faces, theme parks, museums and history in entertainment. None of those would stick in her memory. It would be the little things: The soft jazz that the musician on Los Angeles Street played, the Spider-Mans and Darth Vaders walking down the street, that restaurant that she and Alex went to every day after school. It felt as if she kept on saying goodbye, but how does someone really say goodbye to a city that they've called home for so long?

It wasn't really a goodbye. She just knew it was time to move on. Maybe she would come back someday. For now, it was just her, her backpack and the view of the city from the top of their hill. She and Alex had always sat there, staring up at the sky, admiring the city at night. Out of all the people she was leaving behind, she would miss Alex the most. Alex was her only reason to stay, but Alex had urged her to get out and follow her dreams.

So here she was, on their hill, looking out at the view that was L.A. at night, her last moments in the City of Stars, the city of dreamers, the city of people who want to be successful, a city that she would never belong to, a city that would always be hers. She heard the soft jazz floating out from the city before she escaped, enveloping her in its rhythm, as if it was telling her that they would meet again.

I was inspired by my school and my friends.

Naïve

Rosy cheeks and timid smiles,
sweet words whispered,
the soft sound of the car radio.

Vivid colors on our minds,
despite our nervousness,
shadows played around us,

we gazed ahead.

I've been listening to your songs
your powerful voice,
the echo of your guitar.

Give me your problems, I said,
let them hear our voices.
The City of Angels never seemed so bright.
That moment we were better together,

too naïve to understand.

In the end we'll find our way
back to one another,
always under the same night.

Day Runner

The ineffable tramp of time:
birth — death — repeat.
No purpose, no beauty nor cruelty.
Brackish tears burnish bleached bones.
Marrow molders as a mother's melancholy
wails like siren shrieks.
It makes the mind meander mindlessly
into falsehoods, false imaginings,
unfulfilled dreams that water
the fertile earth to nourish those long dead
their fruitless gains: a moment of fame,
the glimmer of a camera flare.
Neither encapsulated on a tombstone
where their skulls smile for an audience of worms;
flesh folding, faltering,
blood-bruised bloated bodies mocking
"How does so much talent fit into that tiny little thing?"
Ghosts attend the matinee,
pointing at their stars plucked from the sky
and ground into the pavement —
trophies for the tourists to drag their feet on for a moment
before they are reclaimed by the crowd's push
the desire to see a person glitzed and glamoured.
Not a glossy tombstone for
someone whose glitter has since been shed —
the film rolling, clicking to the end of its reel,
grinding to dust all that once was.

The ageless aging agelessly, gracefully gracelessly, run away
wrinkles carved with barbed reviews
and smoothed by the sandpaper of the public eye.
False gentility, tranquility of delusion that the worst is behind.
If the end is the unknown, then the worst is yet unknown.
Fingers are paper folded origami over piano wire,
ink-stained from every touch of a map, a page, a stage,
frostbite-blackened by the end of days,
the stories smudged and smeared
all for nothing, famous smiles beamed eyeless
beneath the block-letter monuments
like ivory teeth: HOLLYWOOD, HERE WE DEVOUR
run, run,
run from the days to come.

Sing. Dance.
Smile. Eat. Love.
Write.

When I left for college out on the East Coast, I was excited to try something new. I didn't realize how lost I'd feel, or how different my upbringing would be from my peers. It wasn't until these experiences that I realized how much I appreciated the neighborhood I grew up in, a neighborhood where everyone was hardworking and always, always proud of their roots. I didn't realize how much I would miss my community center, the solid hands that would help guide us. I come from a neighborhood where everyone is hustling to make ends meet, and before I was ashamed of that. I always tried to hide it, avoided speaking about where I'm from. But today, I consider it an inherent part of my identity. No matter where I am or what I do, I will always call Lafayette Street my beautiful, wonderful home. This poem is a tribute to my street, my roots.

Lafayette Street

I never knew how much I'd miss it.
These people, I miss them —
their voices
accents, like brass knuckles fighting
to be heard.
Their English is remixed
with Spanish
with Korean
with Chinese
with Hindi
with Tagalog —
all mixed into one neighborhood
collectively too big, too rambunctious, too colorful
to be contained.
Even when America tries to wish it away,
it is too beautiful in its noise
its music
to be swept under the rug.
When I was a little girl, I tried to run away
and never look back.
But now,
I find myself always,
always,
listening
for the sounds
of Lafayette Street.

"I can imagine myself as a leader now
after seeing strong, confident women."

— a WriteGirl mentee

15

Never underestimate the power of a girl and her pen!

THIS IS
WriteGirl

" I LOVE WRITEGIRL. IT'S FULL OF KINDNESS, INSPIRATION AND LOVE. WRITEGIRL IS ONE OF MY FAVORITE PLACES TO BE. IT HAS CHANGED MY WRITING SO MUCH, AND, IN TURN, CHANGED ME. "

WriteGirl Publications

BOLDINK

Intensity

www.writegirl.org

WriteGirl is a creative writing and mentoring organization that helps teen girls discover and express their creative voices. Each season, WriteGirl pairs teens with professional women writers for a yearlong program of one-on-one mentoring, creative writing workshops, public readings, publications, and college entrance guidance. Girls develop vital writing, public speaking, leadership and critical thinking skills, and the confidence to succeed in their personal and professional goals.

Founded in Los Angeles by Keren Taylor in 2001, with 30 girls and 30 women writers, **WriteGirl now serves more than 500 teens annually through all of its programs.** Nearly 300 journalists, novelists, poets, TV and film writers, songwriters, and more, volunteer their time and enthusiasm to mentor teens and lead workshops.

WriteGirl teens attend 178 schools throughout Los Angeles County and volunteers are employed by prestigious organizations that include NBCUniversal, 72andSunny, Warner Bros TV, The Walt Disney Company and USC. **WriteGirl volunteers complete a rigorous training program and collectively contribute a total of 3,000 hours each month.**

WriteGirl provides individual college and financial aid guidance to every participant. **For 15 consecutive years, WriteGirl has maintained a 100% success rate of guiding its Core Mentoring Program seniors to graduate from high school and enroll in college.** Many WriteGirl graduates receive scholarships and are the first in their families to attend college.

❝ IT'S GREAT THAT WRITEGIRL OFTEN GIVES US THE CHANCE TO VISIT VENUES WE WOULDN'T GET TO OTHERWISE. ❞

WriteGirl consistently pursues new ways to serve youth. **In 2004, WriteGirl began working with critically at-risk pregnant, parenting and incarcerated teen girls at Los Angeles County Office of Education alternative school sites, including two juvenile detention facilities.** In 2015, WriteGirl recruited and trained men volunteers to create the Bold Ink Writers Program and provide programming for incarcerated boys and co-ed groups, through an alliance with the Arts for Incarcerated Youth Network in partnership with the Los Angeles County Probation Department and Los Angeles County Arts Commission. These partnerships enable WriteGirl to provide creative writing programming and mentorship to an even broader group of constituents, furthering WriteGirl's advocacy work to transform education for system-involved youth.

The impact of WriteGirl is long-term. **WriteGirl alumnae continue to succeed long past college graduation, earning prestigious internships and admittance to graduate programs.** They choose professions that will enable them to confidently lead, serve and make a difference in their communities and throughout the world, in fields that include law, medicine, film, journalism and education.

In the words of WriteGirl alum Lovely Umayam, a graduate of Reed College and a policy analyst with the Stimson Center in Washington, D.C., focusing on nuclear nonproliferation, **"WriteGirl's work goes beyond what you see on paper; it encourages young girls to expand their imagination as writers and as individuals."**

WriteGirl is a project of nonprofit organization Community Partners.

" I LOVED THE SHARING PORTION AT
THE END. IT WAS GREAT TO SEE
HOW COMFORTABLE THE GIRLS
LOOKED AND HOW SUPPORTED
THEY FELT. SOME GIRLS SHARED
VERY DEEP AND PERSONAL STORIES
ABOUT THEIR LIVES. "

WRITEGIRL RECOGNITION

In November 2013, WriteGirl received the National Arts and Humanities Youth Program Award, presented by First Lady Michelle Obama. It is the highest national honor awarded to exemplary after-school and out-of-school time programs from across the country.

NATIONAL ARTS and HUMANITIES YOUTH PROGRAM AWARDS

An initiative of the President's Committee on the Arts & the Humanities

National Arts & Humanities Youth Program Awards is an initiative of the President's Committee on the Arts and the Humanities (PCAH). The President's Committee partners with the Institute of Museum and Library Services (IMLS), National Endowment for the Arts (NEA), and the National Endowment for the Humanities (NEH) to administer the program.

In 2014, WriteGirl Executive Director Keren Taylor was selected as a CNN Hero for her work empowering thousands of teen girls in Los Angeles.

"I thought about how lucky I was to be given this opportunity to represent a program that has helped me achieve not only a passion for writing, but also a confidence that can't be developed from a schoolroom where everyone is in constant competition for the top grade."

— WriteGirl mentee Jacqueline Uy, who was invited to the White House to accept the award

WriteGirl was honored by OvationTV for success in guiding young people into careers in the creative economy. The 2016 Creative Economy innOVATION Grant Award is proudly displayed in our downtown LA office, alongside our other awards and commendations.

WRITEGIRL RECOGNITION

Awards for WriteGirl

2016	The Creative Economy innOVATION Grant Award
2016	Women of Influence Award, L.A. Biz
2014	Keren Taylor named CNN Hero
2013	National Arts & Humanities Youth Program Award, presented by Michelle Obama
2013	Women Making a Difference Award, Los Angeles Business Journal, Finalist
2013	SHero Award for Allison Deegan, WriteGirl Associate Director
2012	Albert R. Rodriguez Civic Legacy Award for Keren Taylor
2011	President's National Youth, Arts and Humanities Program Awards, Finalist
2011	Women Making a Difference Award, Los Angeles Business Journal, Finalist
2010-11	California Nonprofit of the Year by Governor Arnold Schwarzenegger and Maria Shriver
2010	Humanitas Philanthropy Prize
2010	Annenberg Alchemy Leadership Community Champion, Keren Taylor
2010	Ruby Award: Women Helping Women, Soroptimist International
2009	CA Governor and First Lady's Medal for Service, Finalist, Nonprofit Leader
2009	Springfield College School of Human Services Community Hero Award
2008	President's Volunteer Call to Service Award
2008	Community Woman of Achievement, Business & Professional Women Hollywood
2008	Women Making a Difference Award, Los Angeles Business Journal, Finalist
2007	Certificate of Appreciation, Los Angeles Mayor Antonio Villaraigosa
2006	Making a Difference for Women Award, Soroptimist International
2006	Certificate of Achievement, Los Angeles Mayor Antonio Villaraigosa
2006	Governor Arnold Schwarzenegger Commendation Letter
2006	Senator Gilbert Cedillo, 2nd District of CA, Commendation
2006	Gloria Molina, Supervisor, 1st District of California, Commendation
2006	Fabian Nunez, Speaker of the Assembly, Certification of Recognition
2006	Congressman Ed Reyes, 1st District of Los Angeles, Commendation
2005	Certificate of Appreciation, Los Angeles Mayor Antonio Villaraigosa
2004	President's Volunteer Call to Service Award

“ TO WITNESS AN ENTIRE ROOM OF
200 WOMEN SPELLBOUND, SILENT,
AND EXPECTING SUCCESS FROM EACH
AND EVERY BEING IS JUST ABOUT THE
MOST HEARTWARMING EXPERIENCE
I'VE HAD IN A VERY LONG TIME. MY
HEART IS SO FUELED! ”

Kyrsten Sprewell graduated from Tuskegee Institute with a BS and MSW in Social Work; she works in community mental health.

Jeanine Daniels is a creator of online, television and film content as a writer, director, producer and actor; she recently achieved representation from a major Hollywood talent agency.

Fahiya Rashid, a graduate of UC Irvine, is pursuing a Masters in International Relations at Heidelberg University in Germany.

Jessica Frierson, a film graduate of Cal State Fullerton, is a writers' assistant on a new television series.

Woaria Rashid, a communications graduate of Cal State Fullerton, is pursuing a media career.

Jessica Reben, a graduate of Sonoma State as a communications major, is completing real estate school. She hopes to use her license to help international students and all people find housing.

" I LOVE THIS PROGRAM SO MUCH. I HONESTLY DON'T KNOW IF I WOULD HAVE BEEN ABLE TO GET INTO MY DREAM SCHOOL, YALE, WITHOUT IT...

Aisha Holden, a graduate of Cal State Northridge, is a development coordinator at a film production company.

Melina Zuniga, a graduate of Spelman College, is a medical student at the Morehouse School of Medicine.

Lena Brooks, a UC Berkeley graduate, is a filmmaker and theater performer who works for a test prep company.

Glenda Garcia, a Dickinson graduate and Fulbright Fellow, is a law student at Indiana University.

Ariel Edwards-Levy, a graduate of USC, is a reporter and Polling Director at *The Huffington Post*.

Evelyn Hammid, a UC Berkeley graduate, works at a technology media company.

Melani Sutedja, a UC Berkeley graduate, works for a large beverage company.

Lovely Umayam, a Reed College graduate, works in nuclear nonproliferation policy for a think tank.

Gabrielle Gorman is studying Film and Television at UCLA. She is hoping to one day direct feature films that will promote positive depictions of marginalized people. Find her poem in this book on page 242.

...WRITEGIRL HAS HELPED ME BOTH APPLY AND ATTEND THE SCHOOL I FELL IN LOVE WITH AS A CHILD. IT'S ALSO BOLSTERED MY CREATIVITY AND MADE ME A MORE CONFIDENT PERSON. 🙿

Meet Amanda Gorman,
a WriteGirl Alumna

WriteGirl Alumna Amanda Gorman, 19, Youth Poet Laureate of the United States 2017 and Harvard Class of 2020, shares her experiences with WriteGirl and the lessons she learned on finding, and owning, her own voice. Find her poem in this book on page 263.

My hands clammed up as I took the stage, my purple flower headband wrapped around my teeny weeny afro. The first time I read my writing at a WriteGirl workshop was also the first time I'd ever read my work in front of a large audience. Ever. And per usual, my fourteen-year-old self was nervous to recite my poetry due to my speech impediment. My words could look elegant on a page but seemed to lose their eloquence in my mouth. Nevertheless I grabbed the mic, heartened by the unconditional, supportive applause you'll always find at WriteGirl.

I read my poem, and loved the experience! Sharing my work with an audience empowered and energized me in ways I'd never imagined. After that I was officially hooked on performing my poetry aloud as much as I was drawn to seeing it in print. I realized creative writing was as much about words as it was about noise — the beats, rhythms and symphonies created by letters acting as a music sheet in my journal.

After my first WriteGirl workshop, I continued to share my work aloud despite my speech impediment — in cafes, libraries, or living rooms. I came to understand that the specific sound of my poetry — speech impediment and all — made me unique and added even more meaning to my work as a spoken word poet. My dropped r's, my garbled vowels, created the music of my poetry, just as my lengthy lines and my appetite for alliteration formed my own style of written word. That was my VOICE. My accent and style were

Photo credit: Vital Voices

Amanda introduced Secretary Hillary Clinton at the Global Leadership Awards as a HerLead Fellow.

mine to own, and I began to feel proud in the music, poetry, sound and powerful silence my writing and spoken word could generate.

Within a few years, I was performing spoken word poetry around the nation, meeting Michelle Obama at the White House as a Spoken Word Ambassador and named the Inaugural National Youth Poet Laureate this year. While I still get jittery sometimes before reading my work aloud, it is with an energy, confidence and excitement I developed early on performing at WriteGirl.

WriteGirl taught me never to be afraid to have a voice with volume. Whether you're writing in a notebook or speaking to a crowd, with your words you can make some noise, claim the stage or be loud. Celebrate your own unapologetic mic drop moment when your words ring loud and clear. Believe in the worth of your own unique voice, because when a girl with a pen speaks up, she is sure to rock the world.

Adre Yusi is studying English and Media Studies at Kalamazoo College, hoping to write her first fictional novel. She just returned from a semester in Spain and is planning to continue her writing studies in graduate school. Read her poem in this book on page 62.

"WriteGirl has picked me up every single time I have fallen down. Whether it was scrambling to find a scholarship for college, giving me professional advice, or answering an anxious-crying-filled phone call from me, WriteGirl was always there for me. When I was a mentee, Allison Deegan (WriteGirl Associate Director) spent long nights over Skype with me to help me apply to colleges. She was there for all the crying from rejections and there for the happy tears of getting accepted and receiving a full scholarship. I always call or email Allison when eventful things happen in my life. WriteGirl takes care of their alums as much as they do with their teen mentees."

Janel Pineda is studying English and Creative Writing at Dickinson College and studied English for a year at Oxford University. She is hoping to pursue graduate programs in literature and one day become a professor. Read her poem in this book on page 96.

"WriteGirl empowered me in a time when I thought I had no power, and that has allowed me to succeed in ways I never would have thought imaginable. My mentor and friend, Andrea, is someone who continues to actively support my journey as both writer and woman."

Jacqueline Uy is studying at the University of Pennsylvania. She is hoping to attend law school a few years after her undergraduate experience. Find her poem in this book on page 279.

"WriteGirl, above all, gave me a community of empowerment, support and love that I could rely on and could always come back to."

"WHAT I REALLY LOVE ABOUT WRITEGIRL IS LEARNING HOW TO STRENGTHEN MY VOICE IN A WORLD THAT KEEPS TELLING ME NO."

THROUGH WRITEGIRL I HAVE BLOSSOMED AS A WRITER AND A CREATIVE ACTIVIST, AND I HAVE ACHIEVED MUCH CONFIDENCE IN MY PUBLIC SPEAKING.

" I LOVED SEEING OUR GIRLS STANDING IN A CIRCLE. IT WAS BEAUTIFUL TO SEE ALL THE SHAPES, SIZES, COLORS, AGES, ENERGY LEVELS, ETC. OF ALL OF OUR GIRLS. "

WriteGirl matches professional women writers with teen girls for one-on-one mentoring in creative writing. Volunteers are recruited through professional writing organizations, such as the Writers Guild of America, graduate writing programs, book festivals, special events and referrals.

Each year, WriteGirl enrolls accomplished journalists, novelists, poets, editors, TV and film writers, songwriters, marketing professionals, bloggers, business writers and teachers.

WriteGirl screens, selects and trains women writers to prepare them to be effective writing mentors. New volunteers complete two full days of intensive mentor training before working with WriteGirl teens, and mentor advisors provide support and help throughout the year.

Every week, mentoring pairs write at coffee shops, libraries, museums or other creative locations. Pairs write, talk and inspire each other to share their stories and invent new worlds.

Mentoring relationships last throughout the duration of a girl's participation in the program (often four to five years) and many mentoring bonds continue long after the girl has gone on to college.

WORKSHOPS

WriteGirl strives to deliver an innovative and unique experience for the girls in our program. To achieve this goal, WriteGirl continues to build strong relationships with many community partners. Just in the past two years alone, for example, WriteGirl has produced full-day writing workshops at some of the most inspiring civic locations in Los Angeles, including, among others, The Huntington Library, Art Collection, and Botanical Gardens, Dodger Stadium, NBCUniversal, 72andSunny advertising agency, The Hatchery Press, the Writers Guild Theater and The Academy of Motion Picture Arts & Sciences' Linwood Dunn Theater.

Through these relationships, WriteGirl is able to provide a creatively enhanced experience for girls who learn about their community and the world beyond it through an exploration of history, art and culture, with pen in hand.

Workshops are genre-specific covering songwriting, poetry, screenwriting, fiction, creative nonfiction, memoir, advocacy and journalism. Special guests provide insight, writing advice and one-on-one feedback to the girls, introducing them a variety of writing techniques and writing-related careers.

" I LOVE WRITEGIRL BECAUSE THE
TALENT CONTINUES TO ELEVATE.
21ST CENTURY YOUTH WILL BE
BRILLIANT AND INSPIRATIONAL
INNOVATORS OF OUR CULTURE. "

"I LOVED TALKING TO REAL, SUCCESSFUL SONGWRITERS AND HAVING THEM TEACH US ONE-ON-ONE, AND I REALIZED I AM ALREADY A SONGWRITER. IT WAS AWESOME!"

> " I HAD SO MUCH FUN LEARNING ABOUT THE DIFFERENT FORMS OF WRITING ALL YEAR. I NEVER EXPECTED SOMETHING SO AMAZING. "

WORKSHOPS

SPECIAL GUESTS

Journalism

Tamara Duricka
Libby Hill
Seema Mehta
Beverly White
Kateri Wozny

Click: WriteGirl at The Huntington

Jennah Ferrer-Foronda
Joanna Nelius

Creative Nonfiction and Memoir

Charity Hume
Tracy McMillan
Nancy Murphy

College Workshops

Roxana Carrillo
Jamie-Lee Josselyn
Amanda Pendolino

Poetry

Xotchitl Bernejo
Shayne Holtzman
Suzanne Lummis
Felicia Montes

Fiction

Mona Simpson

Songwriting

Joy Autumn
Mikki Brisk
Lauren Christy
Deanna Dellacioppa
Kyler England
Laurie Geltman
Louise Goffin
Kay Hanley
Courtney Harrell
Michelle Lewis
Lisa Loeb
Eleni Mandell
Natalie Meadors
Clare Means
Samantha Nelson
Erika Nuri
Holly Palmer
Shelly Peiken
Maesa Pullman
Priscilla Renea
Bebe Rexha
Lindy Robbins
Janice Robinson
Heidi Rojas
Lindsay Rush
Liz Russo
Pam Sheyne
Jill Sobule
Nat Stevens
Nina Woodford-Wells
Krista Youngs

Screenwriting, TV Writing and Playwriting

Rebecca Addelman
Jane Anderson
Lisa Cholodenko
Jeanine Daniels
Susan Dickes
Rachel Feldman
Jessica Goldstein
Jennifer Hoppe-House
Liz Kruger
Rachel Caris Love
Josann McGibbon
Jamie Pachino
Clare Sera
Robin Shorr
Courtney Turk
Kelley Turk
Jill Weinberger
Maiya Williams

Performance Workshop Leaders

Jessica Hemingway
Aimee McKay
Kelsey Scott

Advocacy, Advertising and Blogging

Erika Bridges
Natasha Crisano
Ali Esterly
Valerie Fernandez
Lauren Ferreira
Michelle Fink
Kiana Garner
Taylor Henriquez
Ellen Lutwak
Alexis Mendoza
Michelle Nam
April Peveteaux
Danielle Rivera
Stephania Silviera
Amie Steir
Camille Yaptinchay

Speakers

Los Angeles County Superintendent of Schools Debra Duardo
Los Angeles City Councilmember Marqueece Harris-Dawson
California State Senator Holly J. Mitchell
Soledad O'Brien
Rosie Rivera

Acting

Keiko Agena
Donielle Artese
Richard Borgia
Wayne Brady
Tracy Burns
Ted Cannon
Mo Collins
Felicia Day
Aasha Davis
Bri Giger
Pamela Guest
Melora Hardin
Tyler Hilton
David Hoffman
Erica Litwin
Tembi Locke
Holly Mandel
Aimee McKay
Wendi McLendon-Covey
Sean McSweeney
Tammy Munro
Carly Pandza
Meghan Park
Shawn Carter Peterson
Vik Sahay
Sherri Saum
Kelsey Scott
Colleen Smith
Ryan Smith
Trevor St. John
Hayden Szeto

“I LOVED HEARING FROM BEVERLY WHITE ABOUT COVERING CRIME AND ASKING HARD-HITTING QUESTIONS ON A DEADLINE.”

“I WISH I'D HAD WRITEGIRL WHEN I WAS IN HIGH SCHOOL.”

SPECIAL GUESTS

PUBLIC READINGS

WriteGirl teens read their work at public events all over Los Angeles. Our girls discover that telling their stories in front of a live audience is fun and empowering.

WriteGirl produces reading events annually at a wide variety of venues, including Skylight Books, Chevalier's Books and the Writers Guild of America Theater.

WriteGirl mentees were invited to the stage at many civic events including The Los Angeles Times Festival of Books, the Southern California Poetry Festival and the Association of Writers & Writing Programs conference.

"WRITEGIRL IS GENUINELY ONE OF THE BEST ASPECTS OF MY LIFE SO FAR. IT HAS OPENED UP AN EXCITING OUTLET THAT ALLOWS ME TO EXPRESS MYSELF CREATIVELY WITHOUT BEING JUDGED. EVERYONE IS SO ENCOURAGING!"

> # "WRITEGIRL IS THE MOST FUN I HAVE EVER HAD IN MY LIFE. EACH WORKSHOP IS SO UNIQUE AND CREATIVE AND UNLIKE ANY PROGRAM I'VE EVER BEEN TO, WITH SO MANY DIFFERENT KINDS OF STIMULUS AND INSPIRATION AND I LOVE IT SO, SO MUCH. "

PUBLIC READINGS

BOLD FUTURES

WriteGirl develops leaders. The WriteGirl Bold Futures Program prepares girls for life beyond high school, weaving together a full slate of college and job preparedness skill building, as well as leadership development, to truly give young women the tools, community, confidence and tenacious communication skills they need to thrive in college, the workplace and in life.

Bold Futures includes an intensive college preparation and attainment program, college guidance workshops, internships, career awareness programs and access to a growing alumnae support network. Volunteer members of WriteGirl's Education Support Team guide teens and their parents through the entire college application process, including understanding and seeking scholarships and financial aid. This unusually intensive coaching is offered in both group and one-on-one sessions, giving girls the full support they need to successfully gain access to higher education.

Throughout the year, you can find WriteGirl juniors and seniors at full-day workshops that focus on SAT prep, college research and application completion, college essay writing and financial aid/scholarship guidance. Girls are encouraged to visit college campuses and apply for scholarships through organizations such as the Posse Foundation. Students nominated by WriteGirl have received full-ride Posse Foundation Scholarships to Grinnell College, Dickinson College, Bucknell University, Kalamazoo College, Hobart and William Smith Colleges, Tulane University, University of Wisconsin-Madison and UCLA. WriteGirls have been accepted at colleges all over the country and the world, from community colleges to the most competitive universities, as well as nearly all campuses of both the University of California and California State University systems.

> ## " I LIKED BEING ABLE TO EXPLORE THE VARIETY OF COLLEGES I NEVER WOULD HAVE THOUGHT TO LOOK AT. THERE IS NO ONE DIRECT PATH. IT'S ABOUT TURNING IT INTO YOUR OWN TRAIL. "

Beyond college, many WriteGirl alumnae are also moving onto advanced studies and professional training, including national and international fellowships such as the Fulbright, and law school, medical school and graduate programs in many fields, including creative writing, journalism, international relations, psychology and women's studies.

Bold Futures also offers intensive opportunities for high school seniors and college students. Interns in the WriteGirl office participate in activities designed to build marketable office and communications skills. Interns work alongside WriteGirl staff and volunteers, taking ownership of projects and receive coaching in accountability, time-management, teamwork, goal setting, project planning and implementation, self-care and work/life balance, resume writing and networking.

Interns help plan WriteGirl creative writing and college workshops, our Season-End event, Poetry Drive, Poetry Paloozas, and Fox Teacher for a Day Event. Interns also participate in career awareness activities and panels featuring special guests such as Los Angeles County District Attorney Jackie Lacey.

The WriteGirl chant is, "Never underestimate the power of a girl and her pen!" We know that the ability to express oneself can empower a young woman throughout her life.

PUBLICATIONS

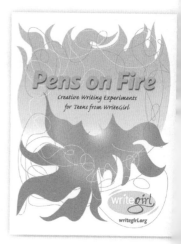

Since 2001, WriteGirl Publications has been producing award-winning anthologies that showcase the bold voices and imaginative insights of women and girls. Unique in both design and content, WriteGirl anthologies present a wide range of personal stories, poetry, essays, scenes and lyrics. WriteGirl inspires readers to find their own creative voices through innovative writing experiments and writing tips from both teens and their mentors.

Fourteen anthologies from WriteGirl showcase the work of over 1,000 women and girls. Selections range from serious to whimsical, personal to political, and heartrending to uplifting. WriteGirl anthologies have collectively won 81 national and international book awards!

Pens on Fire, **WriteGirl's educator's guide, offers over 200 inspiring writing experiments for teens and adults.** Through the innovative use of props, movement, art, music, textures, scents and even flavors, *Pens on Fire* offers step-by-step creative writing curricula for teachers and youth leaders.

ForeWord Reviews, School Library Journal, Kirkus, Los Angeles Times Book Review, The Writer Magazine, Ms. Magazine and *VOYA* have all raved about WriteGirl books.

"Captivating and emotional from the first entry to the last . . ."

— *School Library Journal* review for *You Are Here*

"The creative process is clearly cathartic for the teens and mentors, acting both as an outlet and as a tool to help them make better sense of the world around them. Adolescents reading this anthology will recognize themselves in the words."

— *School Library Journal* review for *No Character Limit*

"For these girls (and their mentors) writing is a lens, a filter, a way to cut through the nonsense and see the possibilities . . . [*Nothing Held Back*] suggests that reports of literacy's death have been greatly exaggerated, that language remains a transformative force . . ."

— David Ulin, *Los Angeles Times Sunday Book Review* for *Nothing Held Back*

Support WriteGirl.
Buy Our Anthologies!

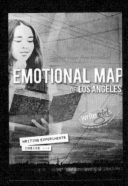

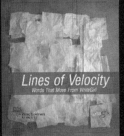

BOLD INK AWARDS

The annual WriteGirl Bold Ink Awards were created to honor the women who inspire our girls, our mentors and audiences around the world. We seek out storytellers whose voices move us. Their genres represent the breadth of our own membership, and their achievements mark the degree of excellence we all strive for. They write in Bold Ink.

Past Bold Ink Award Honorees:

Lisa Cholodenko
Diablo Cody
Wanda Coleman
Liz Craft
Jennifer Crittenden
Kara DioGuardi
Savannah Dooley
Sarah Fain
Janet Fitch
Carol Flint
Naomi Foner
Kami Garcia and
  Margaret Stohl
Winnie Holzman
Zoe Kazan
Callie Khouri
Gigi Levangie
Sandra Tsing Loh
Suzanne Lummis

Aline Brosh McKenna
Nancy Meyers
Patt Morrison
Carol Muske-Dukes
Sonia Nazario
Gina Prince-Bythewood
Lynda Resnick
Melissa Rosenberg
Elizabeth Sarnoff
Carolyn See
Patricia Seyburn
Marisa Silver
Sarah Silverman
Mona Simpson
Jill Soloway
Robin Swicord
Nia Vardalos
Diane Warren

"Everybody is told at some point that they're not good enough. When you keep doing your work, you win."

— Zoe Kazan, Bold Ink Awards Honoree

"THE COMMUNITY IS EXTREMELY WARM AND WELCOMING. I CAN TRULY EXPRESS MY THOUGHTS AND IDEAS AND WRITEGIRL PROVIDES A SAFE ENVIRONMENT TO DO SO. I AM SO GLAD THAT I GOT TO BE A PART OF THIS, AND I'M LOOKING FORWARD TO NEXT SEASON!"

Lights, Camera, WriteGirl! is an annual WriteGirl red carpet benefit. The day begins with a five-hour WriteGirl Character & Dialogue Workshop, where teen writers are guided by their mentors and special guests to craft original characters, monologues and scenes.

One of eight full-day genre workshops throughout the year, WriteGirl's Character & Dialogue workshop is a thrilling chance for teen girls to write alongside Hollywood screenwriters and playwrights.

The evening fundraiser begins with a silent auction, reception and red carpet arrival for guests and celebrities. Celebrated actors bring the girls' writing to life on stage, and a special guest panel of television writers, screenwriters and playwrights discuss each scene after it is performed, making this a highly memorable evening.

Scenes and monologues written by the girls have been performed by Wayne Brady (*The Loud House*), Keiko Agena (*Gilmore Girls*), Aasha Davis (*Friday Night Lights*), Wendi McLendon-Covey (*The Goldbergs*), Tembi Locke (*The Magicians*), Mike Rock (*Black-ish*), Kelsey Scott (*How to Get Away with Murder*), Hayden Szeto (*The Edge of Seventeen*), Ted Cannon (*Party Girl*), Trevor St. John (*Containment*) and Vik Sahay (*Chuck*), among others.

Guest screenwriter/director panelists and workshop leaders have included Rebecca Addelman (*New Girl*), Jane Anderson (*Olive Kitteridge*), Lisa Cholodenko (*Olive Kitteridge*, director; *The Kids Are All Right*, writer/director), Susan Dickes (*American Gothic*), Rachel Feldman (*Beyond the Break*), Jessica Goldstein (*Great News*), Heather Hach Hearne (*Freaky Friday, What to Expect When You're Expecting*, screenwriter; *Legally Blonde: The Musical*, librettist), Jennifer Hoppe-House (*Nurse Jackie*), Josann McGibbon (*Descendants*), Jamie Pachino (*Chicago P.D.*), Sara Parriott (*Descendants*), Clare Sera (*Blended*), Robin Shorr (*The Middle*), Meredith Stiehm (*Homeland*), Courtney Turk and Kelley Turk (*The Secret Life of the American Teenager*), Jill Weinberger (*Chicago Fire*) and Maiya Williams (*The Haunted Hathaways*).

WriteGirl is grateful to the Academy of Motion Picture Arts and Sciences for hosting *Lights, Camera, WriteGirl!* at the Linwood Dunn Theater in Hollywood.

Thank you to RPA, Dream Team Directors and Mini Bites Catering for generous support of this event.

I REALLY ENJOYED WHEN WAYNE BRADY ACTED OUT MY SCENE AND WROTE A POEM ON THE SPOT AND IT RHYMED WAS THE BEST!! IT WAS ONE OF THE BEST DAYS OF MY LIFE.

WRITEGIRL LEADERSHIP

THE WRITEGIRL "ENGINE"

Executive Director
Keren Taylor

Associate Director
Allison Deegan

Communications Manager
Katie Geyer

Curriculum Director
Kirsten Giles

Development Associate
Cindy Collins

Bold Futures Associate
Leslie Awender

Administrative Assistant
Erika Paget

In-Schools Program Associates
Kerry McPherson
Nell Teare
Sharone Williams

Destiny Girls Academy –
WriteGirl Workshop Leader
Jaquita Ta'le

Book Production Manager
Michelle Chahine Sinno

Event Assistants
Zoe Fox
Natalie Meadors
Lindsay Harrie
Jazmine Thompson

Website, Branding, Book Design, Graphics
Sara Apelkvist, Nathalie Gallmeier, Juliana Sankaran-Felix

Photography/Videography
Sheila Cole, Stacy Conner, Katie Geyer, Julie Anne Glover, Luke Grigg, Thomas Hargis, Steven Harrie, Daniel Lir, Mario de Lopez, Daniela Mayock, Breeze Munson, Nicole Ortega, Meaghan Pauline, Jackie Rodman, Marvin Yan

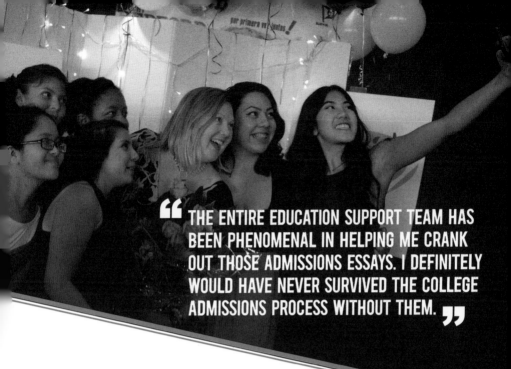

> **THE ENTIRE EDUCATION SUPPORT TEAM HAS BEEN PHENOMENAL IN HELPING ME CRANK OUT THOSE ADMISSIONS ESSAYS. I DEFINITELY WOULD HAVE NEVER SURVIVED THE COLLEGE ADMISSIONS PROCESS WITHOUT THEM.** "

College Interns

Rachelle Aguilera
Pamela Avila
Emily Bradford
Imani Brooks
Madeleine Calvi
Elizabeth Cho
Mumtaj Chokbengboun
Lizeth De La Luz
Rachael Denny
Courtney Hamilton

Morgan Henderson
Lilli Keeve
Julianna Klimeck
Alexa Marks
Crystal Marshall
Eve Mefferd
Kendall Myers
Janel Pineda
Ashlee Polarek
Aunye Scott-Anderson

Madeline Taylor
Jacqueline Uy
Sarah Yanni
Adre Yusi
Nurit Zabludovsky

Special thanks to the Los Angeles County Arts Commission for providing a special summer internship placement for college students at WriteGirl.

High School Interns

Sofia Aguilar
Marie Begel
Mayra Blas
Jessica Bray
Sabrina de Brito
Samantha Campbell
Rebecca Castillo
Valerie Chavez
Angelica Cordova

Vivian Enriquez
Reina Esparza
Luna Garcia
India Glynn
Courtney Hayforth
Anhely Hernandez
Maria Hernandez
Addissyn House
Savannah House

Madeline Moore
Sandra Moore
Sha'Terra Myles
Stephanie Nichols
Marina Orozco
Autumn Victoria

WRITEGIRL LEADERSHIP

WRITEGIRL BOARD

John Marshall: (Board Chair): LSC Communications

Allison Deegan: Los Angeles County Office of Education

Marc Hernandez: Teles Properties

Elise Kroll: Sotarea

Diane Manuel: Urban Wealth Management

Diana Means: Warner Bros. Home Entertainment

Nandita Patel: The Walt Disney Company

Keren Taylor: WriteGirl

Marie Unini: Keller Williams Realty

Sydney Zhang: Capital Group

" THE COLLEGE EVENTS WERE SOOOOOOOOOOOOOOOOOO HELPFUL. "

WRITEGIRL ADVISORY BOARD

Barbara Abercrombie: Writer/Teacher

Shelley Berger: Poet/Teacher

Susie Coelho: HGTV Host and Founder and CEO of Susie Coelho Enterprises Inc.

Mark E. Cull: Writer/Editor; Founder, Red Hen Press

Paul Cummins: President and CEO; Coalition for Engaged Education

Kai EL´ Zabar: Writer/Editor; President and Executive Editor of M2N Publishing/Productions

Elizabeth Forsythe Hailey: Novelist, journalist and playwright

Mollie Gregory: Author/Teacher

Vickie Nam: Writer/Editor, Yell-Oh Girls

Joy Picus: Former LA Councilwoman/Community Organizer

Maria del Pilar O'Cadiz: Research Specialist, UC Irvine School of Education

Debbie Reber: Author

Aleida Rodríguez: Poet/Editor

Diane Siegel: Educational Consultant, Los Angeles Public Library

Caroline Heldman: Associate Professor, Politics, Occidental College

" WORKSHOPS ARE ALWAYS AMAZING. THE STAFF
AND VOLUNTEERS ARE FABULOUS, AND THE
MATERIAL IS ALWAYS ENGAGING AND HELPFUL.
I LOVE HOW PASSIONATE EVERYONE IS. **"**

COMMUNITY CONNECTIONS

PARTICIPATING SCHOOLS:

John Adams Middle School
A.G.B.U. Vatche & Tamar Manoukian High School
Alliance Environmental Science and
  Technology High School
Alliance Judy Ivie Burton Tech High School
Alliance Leichtman-Levine Family Foundation
  Environmental Science High School
Alliance Patti & Peter Neuwirth
  Leadership Academy
Alliance Ted K. Tajima High School
Arcadia High School
The Archer School for Girls
Arena High School
Beechwood School
Belmont High School
Bethany Christian School
Beverly Hills High School
Blair High School
Brentwood School
Bright Star Secondary Charter Academy
Calabasas High School
CALS Charter Middle School
Canoga Park Veterinary and
  Environmental Sciences Magnet
Capistrano Connections Academy
CATCH High School
Chandler School
City Charter School
Claremont High School
Cleveland Charter High School
Cleveland Humanities Magnet
Crenshaw Arts-Technology
  Charter High School
Crossroads School
Culver City High School
Culver City Middle School
Cypress High School
Daniel Pearl Magnet High School
Da Vinci Science
Diamond Bar High School
Eagle Rock High School
Early Entrance Program at Cal State LA
El Camino Real Charter High School
El Segundo High School
El Segundo Middle School
Eleanor Roosevelt High School
Emerson Community Charter School
Environmental & Social Policy
  Magnet High School

Episcopal School of Los Angeles
Fairfax Senior High School
Flintridge Preparatory School
Florida Virtual School
Focus Point Academy
Franklin High School
Gabrielino High School
Glendora High School
Golden Valley High School
Gorman Learning Center
Granada Hills High School
Grand Arts High School
Grover Cleveland Charter High School
Alexander Hamilton Senior High School
Harbor Teacher Preparation Academy
Harvard-Westlake School
Hillside High School
Hollywood High School
Huntington Middle School
Icef Inglewood Middle Charter Academy
Immaculate Heart High School
International Polytechnic High School
International Studies Learning Center
Jeffrey Trail Middle School
John F Kennedy Middle College High Sch
John Adams Middle School
John Burroughs High School
John Burroughs Middle School
John Marshall Senior High School
John Muir Middle School
KIPP Scholar Academy
Los Angeles Center For Enriched Studie
La Canada High School
La Canada Preparatory School
Los Angeles County High School
  for the Arts
LAUSD/USC Media Arts and
  Engineering Magnet
Le Lycee Francais de Los Angeles
Lincoln High School
Linda Esperanza Marquez High School
Los Altos High School
Los Angeles Center for Enriched Studie
Louisville High School
Lux et Veritas Academy
Magnolia Charter High School
Magnolia Science Academy
Manhattan Beach Middle School
Marina Del Rey Middle Schools

Mark Twain Middle School
John Marshall High School
Mayfield Senior School
Robert A. Millikan Middle School
Mira Costa High school
Monrovia High School
Montebello High School
Montessori School of Ojai
New Designs Charter School
New Roads School
New Village Girls Academy
New West Charter School
Newcomb Academy
Notre Dame Academy Girls High School
Notre Dame High School
Oak Park High School
Oak Park Independent
Oaks Christian School
Options for Youth San Gabriel
Orange County School of the Arts (OCSA)
Orthopaedic Hospital Medical
   Magnet High School
Palisades Charter High School
Pacifica Christian High School
Palm Springs High School
Palms Middle School
Palos Verdes High School
Palos Verdes Peninsula High School
Parras Middle School
Pasadena High School
Paul Revere Middle School
Polytechnic High School
Portola Highly Gifted Magnet
Richard Henry Dana Middle School
Ramon C. Cortines School of
   Visual and Performing Arts
Ramona Convent Secondary School
Renaissance Arts Academy
Reseda Senior High School
Richard Henry Dana Middle School
Rio Norte Junior High School
Rosemont Middle School
Saint Francis Xavier School
San Pedro Senior High School
Sandburg Middle School

Santa Clarita Valley International
Santa Fe Middle School
Santa Monica Alternative School House
Santa Monica College
Santa Monica High School
Saugus High School
Sequoia Charter School
Sierra Vista High School
Soledad Enrichment Action Charter High School
South High School
South Hills High School
South Pasadena High School
South Pasadena Middle School
St. Bernard High School
St. John Fisher Elementary School
St. Michael's School
St. Paul High School
St. Timothy School
William Howard Taft Charter High School
Tahquitz High School
Thomas Jefferson Senior High School
Torrance High School
Trabuco Hills High School
Troy High School
UAAS
University High School
USC Hybrid High School
Valencia High School
Valley Academy of Arts and Sciences
Venice High School
View Park Preparatory Accelerated
   Charter School
Vistamar School
Walter Reed Middle School
Warren High School
Westchester Enriched Sciences Magnets
Westchester High School
Westchester Lutheran Middle School
Westchester Secondary Charter School
Westridge School for Girls
Whitney High School
Wildwood School
Glen A. Wilson High School
Woodland Hills Academy
Ynez Elementary School

REFERRING ORGANIZATIONS:

Antioch University Los Angeles
Fox Gives
Idealist
NBCUniversal
Occidental College
UCLA Extension Writers' Program
United Way of Ventura
VolunteerMatch
Writers Guild of America, West

WRITEGIRL SUPPORTERS

WriteGirl would like to thank the following corporations, government agencies, foundations and individuals for their generous support:

Barbara Abercrombie
Adams Family Foundation
The Ahmanson Foundation
Stephanie Allen
Amazon Literary Partnership
American Endowment Foundation
Jane Anderson and Tess Ayers
Vibiana Andrade
Annenberg Foundation
Arts for Incarcerated Youth Network
ASCAP Foundation Irving Caesar Fund
The Bank of America Charitable Foundation
Aimee Bender
Shelley Berger
The Bookworm Box/Colleen Hoover
Bonhams
Maisha Brown
California Community Foundation
California Foundation for
    Stronger Communities
The California Wellness Foundation
The Capital Group Companies
    Charitable Foundation
Paquita Calva
City of Los Angeles, Department of
    Cultural Affairs
Chromatic Inc.
Jody Cohan-French and Family
Cynthia Comsky
Courtside Residents' Association
Crail-Johnson Foundation
Danielle LaPorte Inc.
Allison Deegan
Susan Dickes
DLA Piper Global Law Firm
Brad Dobson and Minette Riordan,
    Path to Profit
Dream Team Directors
Dwight Stuart Youth Fund
Ebell Rest Cottage Association
The Edlow Family Fund
EILEEN FISHER Inc.
The Eisner Foundation
Stephanie Fein
Jennah Ferrer-Foronda
Cameron Foster-Keddie
Elizabeth George Foundation
Frog Crossing Foundation

Terry Gilman, Mysterious
    Galaxy Bookstore
Grainne Godfree
Good Works Foundation
Toni Graphia
Rory Green
The Green Foundation
Sheila Grether-Marion
HBK Investments LLC
The Herb Alpert Foundation
Marc Hernandez
Jennifer Hoppe
Winnie Holzman and Paul Dooley
Rita Hsiao
Kathleen Hughes
The Isambard Kingdom Brunel Society
    of North America
Erica Jamieson
JIB Fund Community Building Initiative
Rebecca Joseph
Journey of the Heart Poetry Project
Joyce Green Family Foundation
J.R. Hyde III Family Foundation
Kathy and Jason Katims
Barbara Katz
Deana Katz
Devon Kelly
Kroger / Ralphs
Elise Kroll
Elizabeth Kruger
Lauren Levine
Los Angeles County Arts Commission
Los Angeles County Office
    of Education
Los Angeles County Probation
    Department
Legacy Collective
Lewis Greenwood Foundation
LSC Communications
Christina Lynch
Diane Manuel
John Marshall
Josann McGibbon
Carol Meadors
Diana Means
Elizabeth Meriwether
Nancy Meyers

We would like to extend a special thank you to Shelley Berger, Rory Green, and Kathy and Jason Katims for hosting unique and memorable events to benefit WriteGirl. Thank you for helping introduce WriteGirl to new friends and supporters.

WRITEGIRL WOULD ALSO LIKE TO THANK

All of our individual donors who have so generously contributed to help WriteGirl grow and help more teen girls each year.

All of WriteGirl's mentors and volunteers for mentoring teen girls as well as contributing professional services, including strategic planning, public relations, event coordination, mentoring management, training and curriculum development, catering, financial management and administrative assistance.

Board members for their support and guidance on strategy, fundraising, communications and development of community partnerships.

Civic leaders: The Honorable Mayor Eric Garcetti, Los Angeles County District Attorney Jackie Lacey, Los Angeles County Supervisor Hilda L. Solis, California State Senator Holly J. Mitchell and Los Angeles City Councilmember Marqueece Harris-Dawson for their support and acknowledgement of WriteGirl's contributions to the community.

All of our inspiring event locations: 72andSunny, the Academy of Motion Picture Arts and Sciences Linwood Dunn Theater, Blankspaces, Chevalier's Books, City of West Hollywood/West Hollywood Library, Factory Place Arts Complex, General Assembly, HNYPT Studios, Impact Hub/LA, Japanese American Cultural and Community Center, Japanese American National Museum, Maker City LA, The National Center for the Preservation of Democracy, NBCUniversal, Pasadena Public Library, Shakespeare Center of Los Angeles, Skylight Books, The Unique Space and Writers Guild of America Theater.

Special thanks to The Huntington Library, Art Collection, and Botanical Gardens for their generous support for workshops and events. Our girls and volunteers gain tremendous inspiration from the art, gardens and staff. The Huntington is an oasis in the city, and we are grateful to bring our members to write in this unique environment. Besties forever!

PowHERful Summit, Exposition Review, GenHERation's Discovery Days, Southern California Poetry Festival and TEDxPasadenaWomen for inviting WriteGirl to participate at special events.

Sara Apelkvist for design and branding strategy, including development of WriteGirl's logo, website, press kit, stationery, book design, promotional materials and ongoing support.

Los Angeles County Office of Education for providing the necessary support to bring our workshops to the teens at Azusa Community Day School, Destiny Girls Academy and the Road to Success Academy at Camp Scott and Camp Scudder, two adjacent detention facilities for teen girls.

NBCUniversal and Ebell Rest Cottage Association for workshop and project supplies.

Writing journals:
Baron Fig, Chronicle Books, Clairefontaine, Compendium Inc., Denik, Exaclair, Fiorentina LLC, Image Connection, International Arrivals, JetPens, Knock Knock, Kikkerland Design, Leuchtturm1917, Paperblanks, Rag and Bone Bindery, Rhodia, Rifle Paper Co., Rock Scissor Paper, Running Rhino & Co./ Madison Park Group, Studio C and Hartley and Marks.

Gift books for our members:
Romy Griepp, HarperCollins Publishers, Marie Kordus, Janet Sternberg and Penguin Books USA.

Food, snacks and beverages at Writegirl workshops and special events:
18 Rabbits, 85C Bakery Cafe - Pasadena, Bagel Factory, Bai5, Big Mango Cafe, Bossa Nova, Buffalo Wild Wings, Cafe Gratitude, Cheeky Home, The Cheese Store of Beverly Hills, Chipotle Mexican Grill, Coco Community, Cucina and Amore, DFV Wines, Dominick's, Green Street Restaurant, Heath and Lejeune, HINT Water, Hubert's Lemonade, Icelandic Glacial Water, Iron Triangle Brewery, Jennifer Pennifer Bakes, K Chocolatier, Katherine Lemon Bars, Kitchen24, La Pizza Loca, Les Macarons Duverger, Little Flower Candy Co., Lundberg Family Farms Rice Chips, Made in Nature, Matchbook Wine, Mendocino Farms, Milk Jar Cookies, Mixed Nuts Inc., Modern Spirits, MOYO, nakedwines.com, Nature's Bakery, Nothing Bundt Cakes, Nutsite, Olive Garden, Papa John's Pizza, Papi's Pizzeria, Porto's Bakery, Riot Grill, Rubio's Coastal Grill, Senor Fish, Sharky's Woodfired Mexican Grill, Spitz, Stella Artois, Stumptown Coffee, Sun-Maid, Superba, The Bagel Broker, The Grain Cafe, This Bar Saves Lives, VOCO, Western Bagel, Yuca's, Yummy Cupcakes (Pasadena) and Zinc Cafe & Market (DTLA).

Mini Bites Catering for delectable food for our annual Lights, Camera, WriteGirl! benefit.

Panda Cares/Panda Express for their longtime support of our annual Character & Monologue Workshop by providing volunteers and delicious food for our members.

Gifts for girls, members and special events:
365 Ltd., Acure Organics, Aesop, Allison Deegan, Areaware, Art of Tea, Buy Love/ Celia Shen, Dermalogica, Discount Mugs, Dr. Bronner's, Earthly Body, Emi-Jay, FACE Stockholm, Financially Wise Women, Generosity Water, Goddess Bar, Heritage 1933, Hi Browsing, Jess' Bee Natural, Keren by Design, Knock Knock, Kristin Rosengren, LA Shares, Liz's Antique Hardware, L'Occitane, Lulu Lemon Athletica, Morphe, Ms. Magazine, Pasadena Magazine, P.F. Candle Co., Playtone, Pulleez International, Purely Elizabeth, Rock Scissor Paper, Rubio's Coastal Grill, Shainsware, Shriver Media, skyn ICELAND, Social Type, Stone & Strand, Tarina Tarantino, Yoga Works.

Printing and copy cervices: Chromatic Lithographers Inc., FedEx Office, LSC Communications

Special thanks to all the generous companies and individuals who donated items for our silent auctions!

" MEETING TEEN WRITERS AND GETTING TO 'OVERHEAR' PARTS OF THEIR LIVES, THOUGHTS AND DREAMS IS MY FAVORITE PART OF WRITEGIRL; I GET CHILLS EVERY TIME WE SAY 'NEVER UNDERESTIMATE THE POWER OF A GIRL AND HER PEN!' I GET TO BE A PART OF GIRLS BECOMING EVEN MORE CONFIDENT IN THEMSELVES AS WRITERS AND AS PEOPLE. IT'S RAD. "

INDEX BY AUTHOR

ABOUT THE EDITORS

Keren Taylor, Executive Director of WriteGirl, has been a community leader for two decades. In 2001, she founded WriteGirl with the idea of pairing women writers with teen girls. Keren has overseen WriteGirl's expansion into a thriving community of women and teen writers and an organization that helps hundreds of Los Angeles girls annually. In November 2013, WriteGirl was honored by First Lady Michelle Obama with the National Arts and Humanities Youth Program Award, the highest national honor awarded to exemplary after-school and out-of-school time programs from across the country. In 2014, Keren was selected as a CNN Hero, recognizing her efforts to leverage the professional skills of women writers to help youth. Working with a team of editors and designers, Keren has directed the production of more than two dozen anthologies of writing by teen girls and their mentors. To date, WriteGirl publications have been awarded 81 national and international book awards. Passionate about helping women and girls, Keren is a popular speaker at conferences and book festivals nationwide. She was selected to serve as a Community Champion and facilitator for the Annenberg Foundation's Alchemy Program, helping guide nonprofit leaders to organizational success. Keren is an assemblage artist and mosaicist. She holds a Bachelor's Degree in International Relations from the University of British Columbia, a Piano Performance Degree from the Royal Conservatory of Music, Toronto, and a Diploma from the American Music and Dramatic Academy, New York City.

Allison Deegan, Ed.D., serves as WriteGirl's Associate Director and as a member of the Advisory Board. In addition, she has served as an Associate Editor on all of WriteGirl's award-winning anthologies. She has extensive experience and expertise in supporting incoming and current college and graduate school students, managing youth and writing programs, creativity and public policy. She serves as a fiscal and policy administrator with the Los Angeles County Office of Education (where she contributed to the development of the Road to Success Academy model for incarcerated youth), and as an adjunct professor in graduate programs at Cal State Long Beach and Trident University, as well as a private admissions consultant. She holds a B.S. from Syracuse University, an MPA in Public Policy from California State University, Long Beach, and an Ed.D. in Educational Leadership, also from CSULB.

ABOUT WRITEGIRL

WriteGirl is a creative writing and mentoring organization in Los Angeles that pairs underserved teen girls with professional women writers for one-on-one mentoring, group workshops and college entrance guidance. Founded by Keren Taylor in 2001, with 30 teen girls and 30 women writers, **WriteGirl now serves more than 500 teens**, annually, through all of its programs. More than 300 journalists, novelists, poets, TV and film writers, songwriters, and more volunteer their time to mentor teens and lead workshops, collectively contributing more than 3,000 hours per month.

WriteGirl has maintained a **15-year, 100% success rate** of guiding the seniors in its Core Mentoring Program to graduate from high school and enroll in college, many with scholarships and as the first in their families to attend college. WriteGirl publishes creative writing by its members in anthologies that have won a total of 81 national and international awards.

Since 2001, WriteGirl has consistently pursued new ways to serve youth. In 2004, WriteGirl expanded its programming to reach critically at-risk pregnant, parenting and incarcerated teen girls at Los Angeles County Office of Education alternative school sites, including juvenile detention facilities. In 2015, WriteGirl began to recruit and train men volunteers to provide programming for incarcerated boys through an ongoing **alliance with the Arts for Incarcerated Youth Network (AIYN)** in partnership with the Los Angeles County Arts Commission and the Los Angeles County Probation Department. Student writing is published in anthologies and participants read their work at culminating events.

In 2013, First Lady Michelle Obama presented WriteGirl with the National Arts and Humanities Youth Program Award, the highest national honor awarded to exemplary after-school and out-of-school time programs from across the country. In 2014, WriteGirl Executive Director Keren Taylor was selected as a CNN Hero, recognizing her creative efforts to help youth and leverage the professional skills of hundreds of women writers.

Through participation in WriteGirl, students develop vital communication skills, self-confidence, critical thinking skills, deeper academic engagement and enhanced creativity for a lifetime of increased opportunities.

Sound Generation: The Resonant Voices of Teen Girls is the 14th anthology from the WriteGirl Core Mentoring Program.

" AT A TIME WHEN I THOUGHT I HAD NO POWER, WRITEGIRL HELPED ME FIND MY VOICE. "

CONNECT WITH WRITEGIRL

Visit our **website**:
writegirl.org

Check out our **blog**:
writegirl.org/blog

Like us on **Facebook**:
facebook.com/WriteGirlOrganization

Follow us on **Goodreads**:
goodreads.com/WriteGirlLA

Add us to **Google+**:
plus.google.com/+WriteGirlOrg

Follow us on **Instagram**:
instagram.com/WriteGirlLA

Follow us on **LinkedIn**:
linkedin.com/company/WriteGirl

Follow us on **Pinterest**:
pinterest.com/WriteGirlLA

Follow us on **Twitter**:
twitter.com/WriteGirlLA

Subscribe to our channel on **YouTube**:
youtube.com/WriteGirlChannel

Never underestimate the power of a girl and her pen.

Keep writing and be kind to yourself.